SACRED WRITINGS

JUDAISM
CHRISTIANITY
ISLAM
CONFUCIANISM
HINDUISM
&
BUDDHISM

EDITED BY JAROSLAV PELIKAN

ON SEARCHING
THE SCRIPTURES—
YOUR OWN
OR SOMEONE ELSE'S

A READER'S GUIDE
TO *SACRED WRITINGS* AND
METHODS OF STUDYING THEM

JAROSLAV PELIKAN

QUALITY PAPERBACK BOOK CLUB
NEW YORK

CONTENTS

PREFACE

Sacred Writings is a response to a widely perceived need for a conve-
nient and nontechnical collection of some of the major Sacred Books
of the major religious traditions. When the set of "The Great Books of
the Western World" was first published in 1952, some critics objected
to the absence of the Bible, which, they said, certainly deserved to be
regarded, by any criterion, as a "great book."

The reply was that everyone could be expected to own a Bible
already. Today that seems much less likely to be true, even for
otherwise quite literate people, with regard to their own scriptures—
in the case of most of us, the Jewish and Christian scriptures. Much less
justification is there for assuming that they even have access to a
Qur'ān or to the Confucian Analects. Yet these Sacred Books and their
counterparts elsewhere are an indispensable lexicon for the understanding of cultures that may once have seemed far away but that today
demand our attention.

When I was asked to undertake the editorship of *Sacred Writings,* my
initial reaction was that it would be fundamentally misleading to put

the Confucian Analects, the Rig Veda, or the Dhammapada alongside Jewish, Christian, and Muslim scriptures as though they were comparable entities, when they are not. The Jewish Scriptures, the Bible of Old and New Testament, and the Qur'ān are, in each case, *the* Sacred Book of the community, while the Confucian Analects, the Rig Veda, and the Dhammapada are each a part of a larger whole. But binding them together in the same set does not necessarily imply that they all have the same standing in the history of their traditions. Indeed, I became convinced that the best way to clarify not only the similarities but the differences was to put them together, both stating the differences and letting them speak for themselves.

I was also wary of trying to take on a kind of "Scriptures of the Human Race." And so let me acknowledge without apology what my own scholarly credentials are and what they are not, and on that basis let me try to be helpful to the reader in making sense of the texts. There are two kinds of scholars who have some right to enter upon such a task. The first consists of those who have made a lifelong study of the history of the major world religions—or, in the slightly old-fashioned term, "comparative religion"—such as my late lamented friends and colleagues, Joachim Wach and Mircea Eliade. The second group of scholars is made up of those who approach the universal through the particular, developing an antenna for the accents of other traditions by learning that no one tradition can be understood on its own terms alone.

My own research and experience have been chiefly in the history of the interpretation of Christian Scripture, which has of course entailed considerable study of Hebrew Scripture also in its own right, as well as some study of Islamic Scripture. On the other hand, for my knowledge of these Confucian, Hindu, and Buddhist texts I am completely dependent on the work of other scholars and have acknowledged that debt in the bibliography. To a scholar whose research has always consisted in the painstaking investigation of original sources in their original languages and then, eventually, in the interpretation of these as a connected narrative of intellectual history, it has been an unusual experience, and a humbling and disquieting one, to have been obliged to summarize and paraphrase the work of other scholars and to have to rely on them so completely as not even to have been able to verify their conclusions by independent study. But having attempted, in *A World Treasury of Modern Religious Thought,* to relate a few thinkers on whom I have worked to their contemporaries on whom I have not, I have attempted in the same spirit to relate to one another the sources on which those thinkers have drawn.

There have been several attempts at putting together collections of the sacred scriptures of humanity. One of the most widely used is Robert O. Ballou's edition of *The Bible of the World,* published in 1939. The most ambitious, still in print after almost a century, is the work of the flamboyant Friedrich Max Müller, the German-born Sanskritist at Oxford, *Sacred Books of the East,* in fifty-one volumes. The list of books that *can* be part of such a collection could, of course, be extended almost to infinity, but there are some that simply *must* be included, or at least whose traditions must be. Adding and subtracting, we have come to six traditions that must be represented on grounds of influence and importance: in the order in which they appear here, Judaism, Christianity, Islam, Confucianism, Hinduism, Buddhism. One criterion that emerged was the desirability of publishing each Sacred Book in its entirety, because even the most judicious selection, being of necessity subjective, can exclude precisely the passages that may turn out to be important in some unforeseen situation. For some of the same reasons, introductory materials have been held to the barest minimum. But because these introductions are important not only to the reader of each individual book but to the reader interested in comparisons, they have been included both in the individual volumes and in this companion volume, *On Searching the Scriptures.*

The titles of the Sacred Books are those that the traditions themselves employ, at any rate when they are using English. For historical dates I have adopted the convention, except of course in quotations from other scholars, of C.E. (Common Era) and B.C.E. (Before the Common Era).

ON SEARCHING
THE SCRIPTURES—
YOUR OWN
OR SOMEONE ELSE'S

A READER'S GUIDE
TO *SACRED WRITINGS* AND
METHODS OF STUDYING THEM

INTRODUCTION

UNDERSTANDEST THOU WHAT THOU READEST?

Most inhabitants of the globe, not only in the past but also in the present, have been adherents of one or another religious tradition. Of these, the vast majority have belonged to or have been shaped by one of the six traditions represented here, namely, Judaism, Christianity, Islam, Confucianism, Hinduism, and Buddhism. *Sacred Writings* seeks to provide decisive and influential sacred texts by which those six traditions may become more intelligible to the serious reader: the Tanakh for Judaism; the Apocrypha and the New Testament for Christianity; the Qur'ān for Islam; the Analects for Confucianism; the Rig Veda for Hinduism; and the Dhammapada for Buddhism.

Although Sigmund Freud may have felt able to dismiss religion in *The Future of an Illusion* as naive and unworthy of rational belief, the real "illusion" may well prove to have been his—the naive expectation of Western secularism that with the advance of science and enlightenment religion would "wither away" (as, according to another secular illusion, the state and the nation were supposed to do after the revolution had established the classless society). For whatever one's

existential or metaphysical attitude toward the phenomenon of religious faith may be, it is a dangerous illusion not to try to comprehend
how it in fact continues to provide hundreds of millions of human
beings with a worldview by which to live and die. Editorial writers,
television anchorpersons, diplomats, and scholars who concern themselves with cultural diversity all too often fail to address the most
fundamental and diverse beliefs in contemporary life until the realities
force themselves on even the most skeptical. On the television screen
we see Catholics and Protestants in Ireland clashing over the authority
of the Pope, among many other things; Jews and Muslims fighting
about the holy city of Jerusalem and the Holy Land, among many
other things; Hindus and Pakistanis and Sikhs disputing one another's
claims to temples and mosques, among many other things; Buddhist
monks in Southeast Asia burning themselves in protest for the sake of
their faith, among many other things. But is it adequate in explaining
these phenomena always to emphasize these "many other things" and
to ignore the persistent component of faith in all of them?

Almost every religious tradition with a sacred book has some
version of this exchange in the New Testament (Acts 8:30–31): the
question, "Understandest thou what thou readest?" and the plaintive
response, "How can I, except some man should guide me?" or, in the
more modern and more inclusive language of the translation employed in this set, "How can I without someone to guide me?"
Significantly, this story answers a question with another question—
also a hallowed religious tradition—and thus leaves the question to
be asked and answered over and over again, as it has been throughout
history. The disciplines, rituals, and lessons through which novices
put themselves to understand their Sacred Book have often taken
quite bizarre forms. But the difficulty of such an obstacle course
increases geometrically if a reader proposes to do what is envisaged
in this set of *Sacred Writings* and takes on six utterly distinct, perhaps
mutually exclusive, Sacred Books with the ambition of being able to

4

give an affirmative answer to the question "Understandest thou what thou readest?" for each of them. This little book intends to be no less ambitious by providing in the first part a brief introduction, employing parallel outlines, for each of the books, and in the second part a few clues to understanding them. Thus it seeks to address and to help correct the often quite astonishing ignorance of many otherwise well-informed moderns about religion, their own or someone else's.

It would certainly be fatuous to claim that reading the Sacred Books in this set will provide the one and only key to such phenomena, but it would be no less fatuous to assume, as many seem to do, that the phenomena are intelligible apart from the faith. Some knowledge of the Sacred Book is, as the philosophers would say, a "necessary" condition even if it is not a "sufficient" condition for an understanding of the culture out of which the book has come and in which it has played a historic role. If, for the readers of this set, such a need to know is true of cultures and beliefs in distant lands, which through modern communication and modern transportation (and modern war) have suddenly become much less distant, it is preeminently true of the beliefs by which those same readers and their own culture have themselves been shaped, regardless of whether any particular reader may or may not lay claim to those beliefs personally. The bloody history of intolerance, persecution, and religious war has, quite understandably, led to the idea that any explosive as volatile as religious beliefs should probably be left alone, at least in public, and therefore that the media and the schools should avoid controversy by agreeing not to talk about it. In their accounts of the controversies of the nineteenth century about slavery and emancipation, consequently, textbooks in American history have sometimes paid scant attention either to the arguments in support of slavery that were based on biblical precedent and precept (such as "the curse of Ham" in the Book of Genesis 9:25–27) or to the moral origins of the antislavery movement not only in the Enlightenment but in the Judaeo-Christian tradition and in its Bible (Mal. 2:10; Gal. 3:28).

If we want to understand one another, or even to understand ourselves, and to know (as is said in the vernacular) "where someone is coming from" on the burning social issues of the day, it is, to put it bluntly, a species of illiteracy not to acquaint ourselves with the texts that have carried such massive authority in different cultures for so many centuries. But today an acquaintance with them may no longer be taken for granted even in the cultures of which they are an integral part. Much less safe is it, therefore, to assume such an acquaintance in cultures to which the Sacred Books of other traditions have been alien, and this just at a time when, at last, schoolchildren and the general public are beginning to realize the cultural and intellectual implications of the discovery that the world is round. The art and sculpture of a culture shaped by Hinduism, the philosophy and social thought of a nation inspired by Islam, or the literature of a people brought up on Christianity are a book locked with seven seals to anyone who has not first opened another Book—in these cases, the Rig Veda, the Qur'ān, and the New Testament. Today, if a public opinion pollster were to ask a representative group of relatively well-informed Americans, "Who said, 'A house divided against itself cannot stand'?" a substantial percentage of those with any answer at all would attribute the quotation to Abraham Lincoln (Springfield, 1858) rather than to the Gospels (Matt. 12:25), from which Lincoln was quoting and which he was able to presuppose as part of the vocabulary of his audience. Even fewer contemporary Americans would pick up the resonances of the Confucian Analects in the sayings of Chairman Mao, or of the Pentateuch in the literature of twentieth-century Zionism, or of the Four Noble Truths of Buddhism in the speeches of Japanese industrialists and labor leaders.

In the present climate of opinion it may be necessary to ask whether such awareness is really very important. The ultimate answer to the question of importance probably depends on one's own faith or lack of faith, for anyone who has profound beliefs of any sort would also regard the beliefs of others as crucial—mistaken perhaps, or even fatal here in time and hereafter in eternity, but certainly not trivial. Yet some understanding of those beliefs would seem also to be crucial for an observer who regards them all as mistaken or deluded. It is only necessary to read a daily newspaper to be convinced that not only realities but also the fantasies and delusions of people can shape their view of the world and their treatment of others in ways that can be either constructive or destructive. Billions of lives are being shaped by the "delusion" of religious belief, and specifically by the tenets set forth in these six Sacred Books. If only to live intelligently in such a world, it ought to be helpful for anyone to read the Sacred Books. By an act of historical imagination we can actually participate up to a certain point in the aspirations and devotions of other times and places. Yet this truly is only up to a certain point, for the curtain is suddenly lowered and we realize with a shock just how far away those places and times really are. That experience has been called "the paradox of understanding." Hence the only way to conclude this introduction is with the questions with which it began: "Understandest thou what thou readest?" and "How can I without someone to guide me?"

I

SOURCES

1

THE TANAKH

Title. The title Tanakh is not really a word but an acronym, bringing together the initial letters in Hebrew of the three principal parts of the Jewish Scriptures: the Pentateuch (*Torah*), which is also known as the Five Books of Moses (Genesis, Exodus, Leviticus, Numbers, Deuteronomy); the Prophets (*Nevi'im*), which includes several of the historical books (Joshua, Judges, I Samuel, II Samuel, I Kings, II Kings), the three Major Prophets (Isaiah, Jeremiah, Ezekiel), and the twelve Minor Prophets (Hosea, Joel, Amos, Obadiah, Jonah, Micah, Nahum, Habakkuk, Zephaniah, Haggai, Zechariah, Malachi); and the Writings (*Kethuvim*), comprising Psalms, Proverbs, Job, the Song of Songs, Ruth, Lamentations, Ecclesiastes, Esther, Daniel, Ezra, Nehemiah, I Chronicles, II Chronicles. (That is also the order in which they appear here, which differs significantly from the sequence in Christian Bibles). The plural "Scriptures" is, therefore, an accurate way to speak about what is in fact a collection of books, not a single book. That is clear also from the origin of our term "Bible": *biblia* means "books" in Greek, but Latin eventually construed the word as a singular, and so do we. For Jews the Tanakh *is* the Bible; for Christians it is the first, and the larger, portion of the Bible, identified as "Old Testament," which presupposes that there is also a "New" Testament.

Composition and Authorship. Of the six volumes in this set of *Sacred Writings,* the collection in the Tanakh spans a far longer period of human history than does any of the others. This is true regardless of when one may date the creation of heaven and earth, for the events recounted in the Tanakh cover entire millennia of the human experience long after the creation. Even the writing of the books themselves took something over a millennium. Most of the books of the Hebrew Scriptures bear the names of the writers to whom they have traditionally been ascribed—Isaiah, Solomon, or Nehemiah, for example. In the case of the Book of Psalms, there are authors given for some individual psalms, such as Moses for Psalm 90 and above all King David for many of them, but no authors for others. By no means all of the books carry any such identification: the historical narratives of Joshua, Judges, I and II Samuel, I and II Kings, and I and II Chronicles are all anonymous. In some instances, most notably that of the Torah itself, the author's name does not appear in the body of the text— which refers to Moses in the third person, as does Julius Caesar in his *Commentaries*—but in the superscription, which may have been added later. The puzzle of authorship has engaged students of this Sacred Book for many centuries, with various candidates being proposed for such anonymous works as the Book of Job. But it has been characteristic of biblical scholarship since the Enlightenment that all the traditional ascriptions of authorship have come under critical scrutiny. In fact, the history of modern biblical criticism among both Jews and Christians in the seventeenth and eighteenth centuries may be said to have begun with the reexamination of the Mosaic authorship of the Torah, which most scholars today would regard as a composite work, the outcome of processes of compilation and revision that went on long after the time of Moses. Controversy continues, not only over the results of this investigation but over the very validity of its methods. But such controversy should not be permitted, as it often has been, to deflect the attention of readers, be they devout or merely curious, from the texts themselves.

Language and Text. In the main, the text of the Tanakh is written in Hebrew (plus a few portions in Aramaic), and it is, practically speaking, the sole surviving body of ancient Hebrew literature. Although it is, obviously, impossible to pronounce any language without vowels or their equivalents, the authoritative Hebrew text itself consists only of consonants. Neophytes in the study of the text learned, as they still do, which vowels to supply where; and around the end of the fifth century C.E. a group of biblical scholars known as "Masoretes" provided a system of vowels written below the Hebrew consonants, resulting in what is now called the Masoretic Text. The editorial work of the Masoretes stood in a long succession of scribes and scholars, described for example in the Book of Ezra, who copied and transmitted the sacred text and sometimes even restored it when it had suffered accidental neglect or deliberate destruction (2 Chron. 34:14–18). The discovery of the Dead Sea Scrolls has made available for the first time significant portions of the Hebrew Bible that antedate the work of the Masoretes by centuries, which has made possible the clarification and correction of various problematic readings. Hebrew is only one of the ancient Semitic tongues, and cognates to biblical words that appear in Ugaritic, Arabic, or other related languages may frequently illumine individual passages. In addition, various ancient translations of the Tanakh—above all the Septuagint translation into Greek (see "Translations" below), reflecting as it does a Hebrew text that is older than any complete text we now have—have served as a source for critical emendation and conjectures about what the "uncorrupted" original might have been. Needless to say, such conjectures, too, have become the occasion for vigorous polemics and discussion.

Canon and Authority. The three divisions of the Tanakh listed above

13

correspond to the successive stages of the process by which the several books acquired normative standing as a "canon." (A fourth division, to be discussed in chapter 2, contains those books that were at one time or another bound together with the "canonical" ones but that did not make it into the final roster for Judaism, although large parts of Christendom did grant them "deuterocanonical" standing.) As the Five Books of Moses, the Torah commanded the earliest, the highest, and the most universal respect, having evolved through the processes of editing and compiling described earlier. It achieved its status as the foundation of the faith and life of the people of Israel by five centuries or so B.C.E. It held that status, moreover, also in communities such as that of the Samaritans, who did not extend recognition to the other component parts of the Tanakh. The assembling of the books of the Prophets (*Nevi'im*), or at any rate of many of them, into an authoritative collection seems to have been going on at the same time as the fixing of the Torah, but scholars tend to date the conclusion of the process after the definition of the Torah, the rejection of their canonicity by the Samaritans being one argument in favor of a somewhat later date. As the very title Writings (*Kethuvim*) suggests, and as the character of the roster of books in this category confirms, these were works that seemed not to belong to either of the first two categories, such as the Book of Psalms (Hebrew *Sefer Tehillim,* "book of praises "). In at least some cases, they seemed so problematic as perhaps not to belong in Scripture at all: the Book of Esther, in which the word "God" does not appear; Ecclesiastes, whose pessimism, despite the ascription to King Solomon, did not seem to fit the tone of biblical religion; and, also attributed to Solomon, the Song of Songs, with its lush and erotic imagery. But eventually—traditionally it was believed to have been around the end of the first century C.E.—all the books now identified as *Kethuvim* were officially accepted by normative Judaism. Within the traditions represented in *Sacred Writings,* the authority of the Tanakh is not confined to the first volume, but belongs directly also to the second as "Old Testament" and contributes to the third. Abraham is "the father of believers" and Moses is the bearer of divine revelation for Judaism in all its branches (as they were also for the Samaritans), for Christianity in all its denominations, and for Islam in all its varieties.

Traditional Interpretation. Canon and interpretation are closely interrelated, and they always have been. To mention the last of the problematic books just discussed, there is considerable reason to believe that the Song of Songs finally qualified for inclusion in the canon of *Kethuvim* because it was already being interpreted as an allegory of the relation of God to the people of Israel, or sometimes perhaps of the mystical relation of God to the soul, for which the relation of bride and bridegroom had frequently been a symbol. Once the Song was acknowledged, its very presence within the sacred canon was a strong argument in favor of such an allegorical and symbolic interpretation. The process of interpretation, moreover, is evidently at work already in the composition and revision of various books. One of the most fundamental of all questions of interpretation, not only for the Tanakh but for all the Sacred Books in this set and indeed everywhere, is the relation between the scriptural text and the tradition of the community (see chapter 7). By an ancient and widely held account, what God delivered to Moses on Mount Sinai was not only the tablets of the Law but a traditional and normative body of interpretation, which has since been transmitted orally. The interpretations that ultimately found their way into the collections of commentary called Mishnah and Talmud represented the ongoing process of applying biblical law to real life, often under unforeseen circumstances such as exile. A special chapter in the history of interpretation deals with biblical eschatology, the threats and promises about the future as a time of divine judgment and redemption. Because a part of the expectation of Israel about that eschatological future came to be bound up with the hope for the coming of the Messiah, Jewish interpretations of the messianic hope both contributed to and clashed with the Christian identification of Jesus of Nazareth as the promised Messiah (Greek *Christos*).

Translations and This Translation. Languages, even sacred languages, have a history; they are born and they die. The Hebrew of the Tanakh lived on as a language of worship and of scholarship, but in everyday life it was largely displaced, in Palestine especially by Aramaic. This necessitated the translation of the Hebrew text into Aramaic (the so-called Targums). Outside Palestine, in the Hellenistic world, the spoken language for many Jews was Greek. In Alexandria, home of the largest Jewish colony beyond the borders of the Holy Land, both the need to make the Bible accessible to Jewish believers who could no longer handle the Hebrew text and the desire to give an account of the Jewish religion to outsiders, interested or hostile, led to the production of the most influential of all translations of the Tanakh, the Greek Septuagint, so named because seventy-two translators were said to have worked on it, each coming up with an identical translation. The inclusion in the Septuagint of books that were not accepted into the Palestinian canon led to the ambiguous status of the deuterocanonical "Apocrypha," which, because Greek-speaking Christians adopted the Septuagint rather than the Hebrew version, became part of the Christian Bible (see chapter 2). For a variety of reasons, the impulses within Judaism that had stimulated the creation of the Septuagint did not produce a continuing tradition of Jewish versions in different languages, and most of the translations of the Tanakh have been Christian. But the Jewish community in the United States—recognizing the same need that had inspired the Septuagint, to make the Bible accessible to a new generation—undertook in 1955 the preparation of a new translation into English, which was completed in installments and finally published by the Jewish Publication Society as a one-volume edition thirty years later, in 1985.

2

THE APOCRYPHA;
THE NEW TESTAMENT

a. The Apocrypha

Title. Volume 2 of *Sacred Writings* contains two collections of Sacred Books that appear only in Christian Bibles. The first section of the volume, "The Apocrypha," appears in some Christian Bibles as an addendum to the books that appear in volume 1, "The Tanakh," which in Christian Bibles bears the identification "Old Testament." The standing of the books included under this category is a highly ambiguous one. That ambiguity, moreover, attends the status of these books throughout their history, as the various names of the collection suggest. "Apocrypha" means "things that are hidden." As the editors of the Apocrypha for the Revised Standard Version of the Bible have summarized the problem, "Some have suggested that the books were 'hidden' or withdrawn from common use because they were deemed to contain mysterious or esoteric lore. . . . Others have suggested that the term was employed by those who held that such books deserved to be 'hidden' because they were spurious or heretical." Another term for them has been "deuterocanonical," indicating that even where they are accepted, they occupy a secondary position in the canon of Christian Scriptures (see "Canon" below). With the titles and in the order in which they appear here, the Apocrypha are: The First Book of Esdras; The Second Book of Esdras; Tobit; Judith; The Rest of the Chapters of the Book of Esther; The Wisdom of Solomon; Ecclesiasticus or The Wisdom of Jesus Son of Sirach; Baruch; A Letter of Jeremiah; The Prayer of Azariah and The Song of the Three; Daniel and Susanna; Daniel, Bel, and the Snake; The Prayer of Manasseh; The First Book of the Maccabees; The Second Book of the Maccabees.

Composition and Authorship. Although these books, in their literary form and style, form a miscellany of Jewish religious literature, there is one characteristic that they have in common, a characteristic that also serves to define their position in the history of the Jewish and Christian Bibles, that is, their relative lateness. They are not only second in rank to the canonical books of the Tanakh/Old Testament, they are also written after most or all of them. As the title indicates, The Rest of the Chapters of the Book of Esther appeared as an addendum to the canonical Esther; The Prayer of Azariah and The Song of the Three, Daniel and Susanna, and Daniel, Bel, and the Snake were similarly addenda to the canonical Daniel. Although they stand as separate books unto themselves, The Wisdom of Solomon and Ecclesiasticus or The Wisdom of Jesus Son of Sirach are collections of sayings and proverbs that have important affinities and continuity with the canonical books of Proverbs and Ecclesiastes. The Books of the Maccabees and I Esdras, on the other hand, approach the historiography of the canonical books of Samuel, Kings, and Chronicles. II Esdras harks back to the apocalyptic tradition of the canonical Ezekiel and Daniel, and it anticipates the apocalypticism of the Book of Revelation in the New Testament. As most introductions to the Apocrypha point out, the one genre of the Tanakh that is missing here is the prophetic. I

Maccabees (9:27) acknowledges that these books come from a time in the history of Israel when "prophets ceased to appear among them."

Language and Text. The differences of scholarly opinion about the original language of the several books of the Apocrypha befit their heterogeneity. Some of them were written in Hebrew or Aramaic (Tobit, Judith, Ecclesiasticus or The Wisdom of Jesus Son of Sirach, Baruch, I Maccabees), whereas others were written in Greek (The Rest of the Chapters of the Book of Esther, The Wisdom of Solomon, II Maccabees). In the case of several of them (I Esdras; A Letter of Jeremiah; The Prayer of Azariah and The Song of the Three; Daniel and Susanna; Daniel, Bel, and the Snake; The Prayer of Manasseh) scholars have found it impossible to decide with any certainty the question of the original language. II Esdras, for example, exists as a Latin translation of an original that seems to have been composed partly in Greek and partly in Hebrew or Aramaic. Except for some Hebrew and Aramaic versions that have been discovered over the past century or so, the Apocrypha survive chiefly as part of the Septuagint, and it is also from that Greek text that they have been translated.

Canon and Authority. The most prominent feature of these books historically, and the one that binds them together, is their dubious canonicity and authority. It does appear anachronistic to speak of a "canon" in connection with the Septuagint; for in it, as well as in the Dead Sea Scrolls discovered in the twentieth century, books that were later to be defined as "canonical" appear alongside others that were not, with no obvious differentiation among them. As chapter 1 pointed out, the eventual canonization of the Tanakh by the Jewish community excluded these dubious books while ultimately including some about which there had been question. But it is a measure of the rapid and all but total alienation between the Jewish and the Christian communities that very few Christians after the end of the first century of the Common Era could read Hebrew, so that effectively the

Septuagint became "the Christian Tanakh"; its readings (and mis-readings) and its "canon" prevailed in the Church. Doubts remained, the strongest doubts being, significantly, those of Christian scholars like Jerome (d. 420 C.E.), who did know Hebrew and who did have associations with Jewish scholarship. Those doubts found a powerful echo in the Protestant Reformers, whose emphasis on the authoritativeness of the original Hebrew and Greek texts of the Bible, inspired by Renaissance humanism, carried over also to the Hebrew canon. It was in response to Protestant criticism that the Roman Catholic Council of Trent in 1546, and then the Eastern Orthodox Synod of Jerusalem in 1672, for the first time made most of the books of the Apocrypha an official part of the Christian canon of the Old Testament.

Traditional Interpretation. The Christian interpretation of the Apocrypha, like the interpretation of the "rest" of the Old Testament, has been decisively affected by the tradition of prophecy and fulfillment. According to this tradition, the history of the New Testament and the subsequent history of the Church are the divine performance of that which had been promised before the coming of Christ. Conversely, the rejection of their canonicity by Protestant Christians caused them to be neglected not only by believers in the pew, but by scholars, and even to be omitted altogether from most printings of the English Bible. From both sides, the sharp antitheses of the Reformation period have softened in recent decades, as the inclusion of the Apocrypha in both the Revised Standard Version and the Revised English Bible indicates.

Translations and This Translation. In a real sense, it is to the accident of translation that many of the books of the Apocrypha owe their very survival, for the Greek Septuagint and then the Latin Vulgate have been responsible for their preservation and circulation. In spite of their rejection of the canonicity and authority of these books, moreover, the biblical translators of the Reformation era did include them in their editions, usually with some warning that they were not worthy of being put on the same level with the canonical Scriptures. (See below, under "The New Testament," for the origins of the translation being included here.)

b. The New Testament

Title. The New Testament is well-nigh universal as the title for the specifically Christian portion of the Scriptures, although such titles as "New Law" also appear in some languages. The word "testament" means "covenant," and is so used in older English translations of the words of Jesus that were the first to be written down (1 Cor. 11:25): "This cup is the new testament in my blood." But the title seems not to have been used about a book—or, again, more precisely a collection of books—until a body of normative Christian writings was placed alongside the body of writings inherited from Judaism. Together these formed a Christian Scripture, made up of the records of the two covenants of God as these had been distinguished by the apostle Paul (2 Cor. 3:6), the "Old Testament" and the "New Testament." Similarly, the word "gospel," meaning "good news," referred first to a message and only later to the fourfold book with which the New Testament opens. The title "scripture," when it appears in the New Testament, obviously refers in most instances only to the "Old Testament," there being no "New Testament" in existence yet; but once there was a Christian Bible with two Testaments, terms like "scripture" and "word of God" came to be applied to this Bible in its entirety.

Composition and Authorship. The oldest and the most numerous books of the New Testament are the letters of the apostle Paul, which traditionally are thirteen in number: Romans, I Corinthians, II Corinthians, Galatians, Ephesians, Philippians, Colossians, I Thessalonians, II Thessalonians, I Timothy, II Timothy, Titus, Philemon.

They are addressed to specific congregations or individuals and usually were written in response to very specific needs and occasions. Distinguished from these as "general letters" or "catholic epistles" are those seven, bearing the names of other leaders of the early church, that were not addressed so specifically: James, I Peter, II Peter, I John, II John, III John, Jude. The "Letter to Hebrews," as it is labeled here, has neither a title nor a writer's name as part of its text, but it received that designation because of its method of argumentation on the basis of an extensive use of the Jewish Scriptures. The four Gospels—or rather, the one Gospel in its four renderings—likewise have no writer's names, but they have traditionally been attributed to Matthew (one of the original twelve disciples of Jesus), John Mark (a disciple of the apostle Peter), Luke ("the doctor" mentioned in Col. 4:14), and John (also one of the twelve). As the account of the life and teachings of Jesus, whom Christian faith identifies as the Messiah or Christ of God and thus as the "founder" in a unique sense (see chapter 10), the Gospels have pride of place within the New Testament. The Acts of the Apostles is a continuation, by the same writer, of the narrative in the Gospel of Luke. The Revelation of John, traditionally ascribed to the writer of the Fourth Gospel and of the three epistles bearing that name, is a Christian apocalypse in the succession of Ezekiel, Daniel, and The Second Book of Esdras.

Language and Text. Although there has been a persistent scholarly rumor about Aramaic originals, particularly for the Gospel of Matthew, the New Testament was written in Greek—not the classical Greek of Plato and Sophocles but the everyday Greek of the Mediterranean world, hence called Koine, meaning "common." Several of the writers of the New Testament, notably Paul, were themselves of Jewish origin; some of the traditions, oral and perhaps written, upon which various of them drew were Aramaic; and most of them knew and used the Septuagint translation of the Old Testament. For all of these reasons, much of the Greek of the New Testament has the strong flavor of translation about it. History has handed down to us none of the original manuscripts of the books of the New Testament, but it has preserved literally thousands of copies in manuscript, together with early quotations from the New Testament and early translations of it. The net result of this process of transmission is a welter of variant readings that, it seems safe to say, is unmatched in the history of Western literature. Coping with these textual variants, the most important of which are reflected in the footnotes of our edition, has been the task of many generations of scholars and scribes, and has helped to develop the science of textual criticism, which has in turn been applied to the editing of the works of other writers, ancient and modern (see chapter 8).

Canon and Authority. Already in the later books of the New Testament there are some indications that the letters of Paul and the sayings of Jesus were being preserved, copied, and circulated as "scripture," but in the absence of a centralized legislative body there appears to have been great variety and a form of local option in the use of such collections. It was, at least in part, the challenge of other writings purporting to be on the same level that provoked from the leaders of the Church some of the earliest compilations of lists of authoritative "apostolic" books. Many of the books now included were on all of those lists; some books, such as Hebrews, James, and Revelation, were in doubt, whereas some that eventually did not qualify, such as the First Letter of Clement and the Letter of Barnabas, did appear in some collections and do appear in some New Testament manuscripts. As authoritative scripture, the New Testament took its place alongside the "Old," but the writings of such Christian leaders as Irenaeus of Lyons at the end of the second century indicate that the process by which its authority acquired universal recognition was part of an evolution in which the authority of the bishop and the authority of tradition were linked to the authority of the Bible.

Traditional Interpretation. That definition of the authority of the

New Testament has also decisively shaped its traditional interpretation, through the circular argument that the creedal and liturgical tradition of the Church was based on the New Testament but that the New Testament was to be interpreted in such a way as to harmonize with the creedal and liturgical tradition of the Church. Because the first part of this argument carried the force that the authority of Scripture was supreme though it was not the sole authority, the interpretation of the Bible has always held a special place in the life and thought, the preaching and worship, of the Christian community. Throughout Christian history, when voices of renewal and reform have been heard, they have come in the name of the original revelation contained in the New Testament, even though their interpretation of it was novel or revolutionary.

Translations and This Translation. The New Testament has been translated into well over a thousand languages, and into some of these many times. Coming as they did at crucial points in the history of their languages, many of these translations have shaped the vocabulary and style of succeeding generations. They have also repeatedly become archaic, with the result that new versions have continued to appear. The English-speaking world has been particularly rich in producing these versions, among which the Authorized ("King James") Version of 1611 has long occupied a position of special honor, even for those who no longer find its language completely intelligible. The translation of the New Testament (and that of the Apocrypha) in these *Sacred Writings* is taken from the Revised English Bible, which appeared in 1989 as a far-reaching revision of the New English Bible, whose New Testament was originally published in 1961. The Revised English Bible was a cooperative venture involving several denominations and many scholars. One of the reasons for its success is that when the scholars had finished their work, the translations were vetted by a group of literary advisers, who tested them for style and idiom.

3

THE QUR'AN

Title. The title Qur'ān, as used here for volume 3 of *Sacred Writings*, is a more accurate transliteration of the original Arabic title than was the older and more familiar English rendering "Koran," because the initial letter in Arabic is a "qāf" rather than a "kāf." Therefore "Qur'ān" has increasingly found acceptance in English usage, being listed in some English dictionaries as a variant of "Koran" but in others now as the first spelling. The word itself means "recitation" in Arabic. The Qur'ān refers to itself as "the Book" (15:1) and as "the Book free of doubt and involution" (2:2). In it God says about the Qur'ān as scripture: "So have We revealed to you the Qur'ān by Our command. You did not know what the Scripture was before, nor (the laws of) faith" (45:52; see also the translator's note to that passage in our edition). Although each of the six Sacred Books in this series occupies a special place in the spirituality of its own community, it is probably fair to say that Islam and the Qur'ān are coextensive in a sense that is not as true for any of the others. As Muhammad Husayn Haykal said of the Prophet: "Upon the Moslems he desperately sought to impress that his humanity was like unto theirs, inspired though he surely was. He knows no miracle save that of the Koran." While we are on the subject of proper titles, there are a few other differences that should probably also be pointed out: "Muhammad" is preferable to "Mohammed" as the transliteration of the Prophet's name and has been coming into general use; "Muslim" should replace "Moslem" as well as the Anglicized Persian or Turkish "Mussulman," not to mention the invidious term "Mohammedan"; and "Allah" in Arabic is the name of the one God, Lord of heaven and earth, not of one god among others, and therefore Christian Arabs employ this title to refer to the trinitarian God in whom they as Christians believe, not merely to the God of the Muslims and the Qur'ān.

Composition and Authorship. The Qur'ān's own answer to the question of its composition and authorship seems, at least on the surface, to be a simple and direct one. As one of the final surahs puts it, "Read, for your Lord is most beneficent, who taught by the pen, taught man what he did not know" (96:3–5). Therefore God did not merely reveal or inspire the Qur'ān; "by the pen" God wrote the Qur'ān, which is, consequently, "only revelation communicated, bestowed on him by the Supreme Intellect" (53:4–5). This passivity of the Prophet in relation to the sovereignty of the divine initiative is a recurring theme in the Qur'ān itself and in the subsequent Muslim tradition. It does not imply, however, that we are completely uninformed about the circumstances of the composition of the Qur'ān. In the apt formulation of Fazlur Rahman, "The Qur'ān is, therefore, purely divine. . . . The Qur'ān is thus pure Divine Word, but, of course, it is equally intimately related to the innermost personality of the Prophet Muhammad whose relationship to it cannot be mechanically conceived like that of a record. The Divine Word flowed through the Prophet's heart." It did so in a series of incandescent divine self-disclosures, beginning in about the year 610 C.E. and continuing to near the end of the Prophet's life in 632. These revelations are, to orthodox Muslim belief, the very voice of God. In them Muhammad was designated "a benevolence to the creatures of the world," whose message it was to say, "This is what has been revealed to me: 'Your God is one and only God'" (21:107–8). Muhammad memorized many of these sayings, as did a multitude of his followers; other sayings seem to have been written down right away, in whatever medium was at hand. The collecting of the Qur'ān is attributed to Abū Bakr, the first caliph, and the standard version to 'Uthmān, the third caliph, who established the textual tradition at Medina as the normative one and who also fixed the sequence of the 114 surahs, more or less from the longest to the shortest. Many Western scholars tend to think that the Qur'ān in its present form began to be set down about 650 C.E., but that the text was not definitively fixed until the tenth century of the Common Era.

Language and Text. The Qur'ān is written in Arabic, which thereby became a sacred language, even for those Muslims who are not Arabs. As Muhammad Abduh said, "In the early epoch of Islam, scholars . . . came to the conclusion that the faith will not endure without the Koran. To this verdict further confirmation was added when the intermingling of the Arab with other races was under way. Like their Arab coreligionists, foreign converts to Islam came to appreciate the imperative need to retain the integrity of the Arabic language." It is specifically this Arabic Qur'ān that is identified by God as "the immaculate Book" (12:1–3), and no translation of it into any language can lay claim to a status in any way approaching the Arabic original (see also "Translations" below). Although Arabic, spoken and written, has naturally continued to evolve as a language, or really as several languages in various parts of the Middle East, "classical" Arabic continues to be defined, both by Muslims and by Western scholars, first of all in Qur'ānic terms. Muslim grammars, lexicons, and other linguistic aids for classical Arabic have sometimes tended to restrict themselves to the sacred text itself, with a corresponding suspicion toward parallels from other languages, literatures, and religions. Because of the reverence for it as verbally inspired, the transmission of the Arabic text, once this was fixed, has been carried out by Muslim scribes over the centuries with great care (see also chapter 9). That reverence, combined as it is with a revulsion from idolatry and from anthropomorphic depictions of the Divine in any form, has been responsible for the creativity of Arabic calligraphy, samples of which are visible in the margins of our edition.

Canon and Authority. The authority of the Qur'ān is the authority of the Prophet, which is the authority of God. "O you who believe," it declares, "obey God and the Prophet, and do not waste your deeds" (47:33). To be a believer and not to waste one's deeds means to find in the authoritative Qur'ān, correctly interpreted and properly understood, and in the light of reason, all the instruction and guidance needed for the concrete decisions of life. But because the Qur'ān—like the Torah of the Jewish Tanakh, but unlike the Christian New Testament—contains many specific "theocratic" provisions about the ordering of political, social, and economic life for a whole nation and its rulers as well as their subjects, its authority has direct and immediate bearing on the entire fabric of existence, corporate as well as individual; in the Qur'ān "all affairs are sorted out and decided as commands" from God (44:4–5). Therefore the Qur'ān legislates specific ordinances for marriage, sex, and divorce; it has much to say about slavery and war; and it prescribes rules of procedure for law courts and trials, "civil" as well as "ecclesiastical." The history of Islamic civilization in the more than thirteen centuries counted by the Muslim calendar (which begins with 16 July 622 C.E., the date of the Hegira of Muhammad from Mecca to Medina) provides rich documentation of the applicability of the Qur'ān's authority across an enormous spectrum of social structures in Europe, Asia, and Africa. The efforts to apply that authority with greater rigor to various societies have constituted a portentous new chapter in the history of the final decades of the twentieth century.

Traditional Interpretation. The high doctrine of the origin and authority of the Qur'ān, like analogous doctrines of biblical inspiration in other faiths, could lead to diametrically opposed systems of interpretation. It could be taken to imply either that the task of later generations consisted of determining as precisely as possible what the text meant and adhering strictly to that meaning, or that the determination of such a meaning should serve as the basis to elaborate an extension of the sense to its very limits. Sunni and Shi'a, the two great sectarian divisions within Islam—which are, in the first instance, defined by the question of whether the legitimate succession from the Prophet lies with the first four caliphs, as Sunni Muslims hold, or whether it lies with Ali, the son-in-law of Muhammad, and with the divinely inspired imams whom God has appointed to follow him, as Shi'ite Muslims teach—diverge also on this issue of the proper methodology for the traditional interpretation of the Qur'ān. "In its simplest manifestation," as Edward J. Jurji has described it, "the cleavage here rested on whether *tawil* (interpretation) was to be made synonymous with *tafsir* (exegesis), following the Koran and the Tradition, as the Sunnites maintained, or to be turned into an allegorical exposition, capable of wringing from the text far-reaching implications concealed from the reader, in the Shiite style." In addition, the tradition of ascetic mysticism usually identified as Sūfī, whose best-known and most influential spokesman was probably the medieval writer al-Ghazālī (d. 1111 C.E.), developed its own special method of interpreting the Qur'ān as a mystical rather than merely a legal text.

Translations and This Translation. The privileged position accorded to Arabic as the sacred language has led, as a direct corollary, to a profound hesitancy about rendering the text of the Qur'ān into any other language, even into the languages of the Islamic peoples themselves, such as Urdu or Persian, much less into those of the outside world. Such translations have nevertheless repeatedly appeared. Thus it was at the behest of Peter the Venerable, the abbot of the monastery at Cluny, that the Qur'ān was translated into Latin for the first time, in 1143. This Latin translation and those that followed sometimes served as the basis for versions in other Western tongues, but the scholarly study of Arabic at Western universities since the eighteenth century has made it possible to produce translations directly from the original. George Sale (d. 1736), one of the British scholars responsible for the translation of the New Testament into Arabic, was also the first to translate the Qur'ān directly from Arabic into English (1734). The present translation is the work of the Pakistani man of letters Ahmed Ali, whose collection and translation of Urdu poetry, *The Golden Tradition*, has been widely received in the West. For reasons that have already been stated, the Qur'ān is being presented here in a bilingual edition, with the original Arabic in the margins alongside the corresponding lines in English.

4

THE ANALECTS OF CONFUCIUS

Title. A majority of the titles being used here for the Sacred Books (Tanakh, Qur'ān, Rig Veda, Dhammapada) are transliterations, more or less, from the original languages in which those works were composed: Hebrew, Arabic, Sanskrit, and Pali. By contrast, the term "Analects," which has, thanks to the work of James Legge (see "Translations" below), come to be so totally identified with Confucianism that it is seldom met with anymore in any other context, is, of all things, a Greek word, referring to any miscellaneous collection and then specifically to a literary one. Thus the *Oxford English Dictionary* renders it as: "Literary gleanings; collections of fragments or extracts. (Usually as a title)," and then refers to Confucius. The Chinese title is *Lun Yü*, which means, as our translator here, Arthur Waley, renders it, "Selected Sayings," so that "Analects" proves to be still a reasonably acceptable equivalent in English. Several translators and commentators have pointed out that the first part of the title, the word *Lun*, appears within the text of the Analects itself (14:9), where it refers to the process of editing a document. As Benjamin I. Schwartz has put it,

"The consensus among modern scholars is that our most reliable source for the early Confucian school, if not for the vision of the master himself, is the collection of brief dialogues and gnomic utterances in the collection called in Chinese the *Lun-Yü*, translated by Legge as *Analects*, and by Waley as 'Selected Sayings.'" The name "Confucius" is also of Western origin, being a Latinized form of the Chinese K'ung Fu-tzu.

Composition and Authorship. According to the generally accepted chronology, about which some scholars have nevertheless raised questions, Confucius was born in 551 B.C.E. and died in 479. As is true of several other Sacred Books in this series, the composition of the Analects may be said to have taken place in two stages, oral and written. In one sense they were composed in the course of their being spoken, supposedly by Confucius himself. The debates that have raged among scholars about the authenticity of the sayings attributed to Jesus in the Gospels, or for that matter to Socrates in the dialogues of Plato, have their counterpart here in the study of the Analects. Thus our translator is sure, commenting on Analects 13:3, that "the whole of this highly elaborate, literary paragraph bears the stamp of comparatively late date." According to the text itself, in a passage to which the commentators have given a great deal of attention, "The Master seldom spoke of profit or fate or Goodness" (9:1). But in fact there is much in the Analects at any rate about Goodness. Many of the sayings appear as answers to questions that are put to Confucius by one or another of his disciples or by a critic. The same question can come from more than one source, with each of the Master's replies carrying a distinct nuance (2:5–8). Sometimes, we are told, these questions were meant "half playfully," and his response came "in the same playful spirit" (6:24). On the other hand, many of the sayings seem to have been composed as free discourse, without direct provocation. And some sayings (e.g., 19:17–18) explicitly take the form of secondary quotations by later scribes, while Books 10 and 20 are, in the main, not primarily attributed to him. From these we may begin to surmise something about the process of "composition" in the second sense, the writing down and collecting of sayings and stories by various of the students whose names—though often little or nothing else—we know from the pages of the Analects.

Language and Text. Being a compilation from what seems to have been such a broad range of sources, oral as well as written, the Analects existed in widely variant texts long after the death of the Master. From historical accounts it appears that, in addition to the standard version generally identified as that of "the state of Lu," there were in the second century B.C.E. at least two others, both of which have since been lost: an ancient script version, divided into twenty-one books, and the version of "the state of Ch'i," divided into twenty-two books. Modern critical scholars have suggested, quite plausibly, that many of the individual sayings and maxims preserved in the Analects have acquired, in the course of repetition and interpretation, explanatory contexts after the fact, and that therefore the answers attributed to Confucius in the text may in fact have been older than the questions attributed to his disciples. Once it was set in its present form, however, the text of the Analects appears to have been the object of the same kind of tender loving care that has been invested in the texts of the other Sacred Books collected in these *Sacred Writings*. Like those other Sacred Books, the Analects is replete with archaic and technical terms, over whose explication Confucian scholars and Western Sinologists have expended great effort, none more laborious than that of translators compelled to find equivalents in a linguistic, philosophical, and religious tradition altogether alien to the language and spirit of the Chinese of the Analects. But even native-born Chinese scholars describe how they have puzzled over single words and individual ideograms that seem to bear no connection to present-day language. For that reason among others we have, in the case of the Analects, included the translator's introduction, additional notes and textual notes.

Canon and Authority. Once again with a caveat about not applying uncritically the special connotations with which the term "canon" is freighted in Western usage, especially in Christian usage, it is necessary to locate the Analects within the total context of the canon of "the Chinese Classics," of which it is only one, albeit the one that is the most familiar to Western readers. The most comprehensive list embraces thirteen titles, which in their Chinese titles (and English translations of the titles, as given by Wing-Tsit Chan) are: *I Ching*, "Classic of Changes"; *Shu Ching*, "Classic of History"; *Shih Ching*, "Classic of Poetry"; *Chou li*, "Rites of Chou"; *I li*, "Ceremonies and Rituals"; *Li chi*, "Record of Rites"; *Tso chuan*, "Tso's Commentary"; *Kung-yang chuan*, "Kung-yang's Commentary"; *Ku-liang chuan*, "Ku-liang's Commentary"; *Lun Yü*, "Analects"; *Hsiao Ching*, "Classic of Filial Piety"; *Erh ya*, "Near to Correctness," a dictionary; and *Meng-tzu*, "Mencius," which is the Latinized form of the name of a Chinese sage from the fourth century B.C.E. Although the Analects do not belong to the shorter lists of the Five, the Six, or the Nine Chinese Classics, their particular appeal, and in this sense a special authority, stems from their presenting the "sayings of the Master"—a title that could be and has been applied as well to Deuteronomy, the Four Gospels, the Qur'ān, and the Dhammapada. Confucian tradition credits Confucius with having assembled and edited several of these "Classics." Here in the Analects, moreover, the Master says of himself, "I am simply one who loves the past and who is diligent in investigating it" (7:19). There are repeated references to "the Books" (e.g., 14:43), ancient writings whose authority the Master seems to acknowledge and to whose explication he applies himself, his interpretation thereby having become normative.

Traditional Interpretation. It would seem that there is no more appropriate way to address this question than to repeat the summary of recent scholarship by the translator of the Analects in this edition, Arthur Waley: "There are two main interpretations of the *Analects*,

34

the 'old' and the 'new.' The old interpretation is that of the *Lun Yü Chi Chieh*, 'Collected Explanations of the *Lun Yü*,' presented to the throne by a committee of scholars about A.D. 240. . . . The old interpretation, in all its essentials at any rate, held the field until the second half of the twelfth century. Hitherto the *Analects* had been a scripture among other scriptures, studied by those who were adept in ancient literature. But in the Sung dynasty it became a school-book, and finally not merely *a* school-book, but *the* school-book, basis of all education. This transformation was due almost entirely to the efforts of one very remarkable man, Chu Hsi (A.D. 1130–1200). . . . Chu Hsi has been called a great scholar, but no one would call him so who had any experience of the difference between scholarship and theology. For though Chu Hsi was not a theologian in the literal sense of the term, though he is concerned with a Truth rather than with a God, his methods are at every point those of the theologian, not those of the scholar. It was not his aim to discover, as a scholar would have done, what the Classics meant when they were written. . . . Chu Hsi's task was to make this hidden Truth, ensconced in the Classical books, accessible to everybody."

Translations and This Translation. By far the most influential translation of Confucius into English—in the opinion of some scholars, the most influential into any Western language—was that of James Legge, who, after having been a missionary to the Chinese and the head of the Anglo-Chinese College in Hong Kong, where he lived for thirty years, became the first professor of Chinese at Oxford. Between 1861 and 1886 Legge published a massive translation of the *Chinese Classics*, with introductions, notes, and commentaries, in twenty-eight volumes. With the exception of the monumental work edited by Max Müller, *Sacred Books of the East* (see chapter 5, under "Language and Text"), to which Legge contributed the six volumes of "The Sacred Books of China," Legge's work is unmatched for scope and ambition, before or since, and his rendering of the Analects is the one on which generations of English-speaking students have been reared. While acknowledging his own debt to Legge, Arthur Waley, previously known best for his translation of the *Tale of Genji*, has produced in the present translation a fresh new reading, which, as he puts it, "attempts to tell the European reader not what the book means to the Far East of to-day, but what it meant to those who compiled it."

5

THE RIG VEDA

Title. The title Rig Veda has long since permanently established itself in English usage, whether scholarly or popular. From time to time there have been slight variations in transliteration and in the use of diacritical marks for the Sanskrit characters, including the rendering "Ṛgveda" employed by Griffith for the translation we are using. An early reference to the Rig Veda in English, dated 1776, identifies it as "the Reig Beid," but soon thereafter it was being called "the Rig-véda." The more complete official title is *Rig Veda Samhitā*. The Sanskrit word *veda* means "knowledge," especially sacred knowledge, and therefore might in some ways be rendered more appropriately with the English word "wisdom." In modern Slovak, my mother tongue, *veda* is still the word for "knowledge," and the Indo-European root is also reflected in *wissen*, the German verb "to know," as well as in the English word *wit*. "Veda" is used as the title not only for Rig Veda, but for the other three primary books of revelation in Hinduism: Yajur Veda, Sāma Veda, and Atharva Veda (see "Canon" below). Among the four, the Rig Veda is, in the words of our translator, Ralph

T. H. Griffith, "the oldest, the most important, and the most generally interesting." *Rig* is a transliteration, more or less accurate, of the Sanskrit word for "praise"; it appears to be a reflection of the central place occupied here by the element of praise and prayer, "Mantra," which together with its correlative of "Brahmana" ("critical reflection" or "rational contemplation") may be said to constitute the core of Vedic religion and philosophy, especially that of the Rig Veda: "The sages make their voices heard with hymns" (10:64.15).

Composition and Authorship. There are just over one thousand hymns in the Rig Veda, comprising a total of something more than ten thousand verses. Although some collections of the Rig Veda in the tradition of India have based their groupings of its verses on a distribution creating eight sections of roughly equal length, the principle followed here has sought to employ the historic origins of the material as the basis for the grouping, which has produced the ten books offered here. As the notes to the present edition indicate, the Hindu religious and literary tradition has identified some of the seers to whom it ascribes the composition, under the sway of divine inspiration, of various of the Vedic hymns. Thus there are in Book 1 sixteen such seers altogether, the first two hymns being attributed to "Madhucchandās Vaiśvāmitra, a son or descendant of the famous Viśvāmitra," the hymns from the twelfth to the twenty-third inclusive to "Medhātithi, son of Kanva," and so on. Sanskritists are largely in agreement, however, that many, perhaps most, of these hymns, like their counterparts in others of the traditions represented in these *Sacred Writings*, were both composed orally and transmitted orally long before being set down in written form; to the present day they are memorized and recited by devout Hindus as oral tradition. That oral emphasis is indicated by the very use of the general title "śruti" ("that which was heard") for the collection of the four Vedas, and it is reflected, for example, in such a formula as this: "O Indra, Lord of Hundred Powers, with all our songs we invoke Thy names"

38

(3:37.3). The identification of the writers as "seers," moreover, emphasizes their passive role as instruments for the several deities whose praises the Rig Veda sings, which must significantly modify the use of a modern and secular term like "author" for them: "These holy songs he [Indra] taught the bard who praised him" (3:34.5). Because of the strict requirement that the hymns be recited with precise observance of every detail, and with the rituals attending the recitation being scrupulously followed (e.g., 8:31.1–2), the composition—or compilation—of the Rig Veda and its related materials must be understood in the light of the liturgical requirements of the older Vedic religion and of the Brahmanism and Hinduism that succeeded it.

Language and Text. The language of the Rig Veda is usually identified as a dialect of archaic Sanskrit, for which it and the other three Vedas form the principal corpus of literature. Because of its vital importance as the oldest Indo-European language for which a large body of written literature has been preserved, Sanskrit (and the Vedic dialect in connection with it) is seen as fundamental to the history of all the Indo-European language families. As a consequence of its linguistic interest, therefore, the Rig Veda has been the object of intense attention not only from scholars of India or of Hindu religion and philosophy, but from scholars of Greek, Latin, Germanic, and Slavic comparative philology. Sanskrit grammars and lexicons, intended principally for students of linguistics, may often illumine the religious and liturgical significance of individual passages in the Rig Veda, as the editor's notes to many of the hymns (e.g., 7:97) make clear. There nevertheless remain many difficulties, linguistic as well as textual, for both Eastern and Western scholars (see, as one example among many, 8:52.1, with the translator's note).

In any consideration of the language and text of the Rig Veda, it is impossible not to speak about the work of one of the most widely celebrated of modern scholars and popularizers in the history of religions, Friedrich Max Müller. Max Müller is best known for editing the fifty-one volume *Sacred Books of the East*, published by the Claren-don Press between 1879 and 1910, a collection of, as he himself described them, "translations of all the most important works of the seven non-Christian religions [, which] have exercised a profound influence on the civilizations of the continent of Asia." Less well known to the general public was his work as editor of the Sanskrit text of the Rig Veda in six volumes, which came out between 1849 and 1874. Vedic scholars both in India and in the West have expressed their admiration for this edition, because he established the original text of the Rig Veda in accordance with the canons of critical philology. It was Max Müller's edition that served as the basis of the present translation by Ralph T. H. Griffith (see "Translations" below).

Canon and Authority. The Rig Veda is the oldest of the four Vedas that comprise the central "canon" of the older Vedic religion and of the Brahmanism that emerged from it, the other three being, as already mentioned: Yajur Veda, Sāma Veda, and Atharva Veda. The four Vedas taken together, as Joseph Mitsuo Kitagawa has summarized their position, "constitute the 'revealed' ('Śruti,' or 'that which was heard') literature, and they provide the basis of religious authority in Hindu orthodoxy." But it is in keeping with the genius of Hinduism, as Kitagawa immediately goes on to point out, that it "has never insisted on the acceptance of any one interpretation of its doctrines" and that therefore such a term as his phrase "religious authority in Hindu orthodoxy" must not be understood according to Western theological categories. Nevertheless, what makes the Rig Veda part of that "canon" and invests it with that "authority" is its very adaptability to the Hindu refusal to fix a creed or dogma. In a familiar formula from Book 1 of the Rig Veda, which has often been quoted by those who would interpret Hindu religion as implicitly monotheistic, "They call him Indra, Mitra, Varuna, Agni, and he is heavenly nobly-winged Garutmān. To what is One, sages give many a title: they call it Agni, Yama, Mātariśvan" (1:164.46). To understand the authority of the Rig

40

Veda, it is also necessary to keep constantly in mind its location within the body of Sanskrit literature (see chapter 11); for not only does it, especially in its later books, contain elements that strike the outside reader as "secular"—a term that is at best anachronistic in this context—but the Rig Veda and the other Vedas occupy a place in the national culture that is analogous in some respects to that of the several epics in various other national literatures, including the Greek and the Nordic.

Traditional Interpretation. The distinction mentioned earlier, between Mantra as praise and prayer and Brahmana as critical reflection or rational contemplation, has also shaped the traditional interpretation of the Rig Veda. The Brahmanas are normative commentaries on the several Vedas, explaining in prose the imagery of the Vedic hymns and prescribing ritual, while Aranyakas, a title usually translated as "Forest Texts," present interpretations of the Mantras and of ritual that are sometimes characterized as "mystical." The most widely known of the commentaries, which are in fact compositions in their own right, are the Upanishads, in which the language of the Vedas serves as the basis for cosmological and philosophical ideas that are in some respects already anticipated here in the Rig Veda (see 3:54.8, and the translator's note there). The designation of the Vedas, Brahmanas, Aranyakas, and Upanishads as "śruti" forms of revelation has its counterpart in the body of Sanskrit literature called "smriti," meaning "that which is remembered," of which the best known to Western readers is the Bhagavad Gita. As is the case with other Sacred Books, such as the Tanakh and the Qur'ān, the eminence of these books as monuments of the culture of India means that they form part of the education even of those who do not conform to the orthodox tradition. For example, when Mohandas K. Gandhi was growing up, as he says in his autobiography, he "read with interest Max Müller's book, *India— What Can It Teach Us?* and the translation of the *Upanishads* published by the Theosophical Society"; that reading, Mahatma Gandhi continues, "enhanced my regard for Hinduism, and its beauties began to grow upon me. It did not, however, prejudice me against other religions."

Translations and This Translation. Horace Hayman Wilson, professor of Sanskrit at Oxford and author of a *Sanskrit-English Dictionary* published in 1819, undertook a translation of large parts of the Rig Veda into English, which began to appear in 1850. But Friedrich Max Müller's work on the original Sanskrit text of the Rig Veda made it possible for Ralph T. H. Griffith to prepare a complete English translation, whose preface is dated 25 May 1889. He published an improved edition in 1896. So well established has Griffith's rendition of the Rig Veda become that it was taken as the basis for the modern Indian edition of the Rig Veda in English, published at Delhi in 1973 and again in 1976. For these reasons, and because it presents the complete Rig Veda rather than merely selections from it, the Griffith version is the one being presented here, but the reader should be aware that there are several renderings of such selections into English, among which the sprightly and erudite collection by Wendy Doniger O'Flaherty for Penguin Books is especially appealing.

6

THE DHAMMAPADA

Title. The Dhammapada is undoubtedly the least familiar of all the titles of Sacred Books in this set. It is also perhaps the most obscure in its original meaning, as both Buddhist scholars and Western Buddhologists have acknowledged. The two parts of the compound word are "dhamma" and "pada." As Friedrich Max Müller explained in the introduction to his translation of the work in *Sacred Books of the East*, first published in 1881: "'Dhamma' has many meanings. Under one aspect it means religion, particularly the religion taught by Buddha, the law which every Buddhist should accept and observe. Under another aspect 'dhamma' is virtue, or the realisation of the law." The word "pada" is interpreted more explicitly in the text of the Dhammapada itself: "The path to the Deathless is awareness; unawareness, the path of death" (21). As the commentary explains, "the path: *padam*" refers to "the means, the way." Max Müller suggested the translation "footstep of religion," but added that "it cannot be denied that the title of Dhammapada was very soon understood in a different sense also, namely, as 'Sentences of Religion.'" The translators of our

43

version here, John Ross Carter and Mahinda Palihawadana, propose: "The title *Dhammapada* means 'sayings of dhamma'—that is, religiously inspiring statements thought to have been made by the Buddha on various occasions." They go on to explain: "The word 'dhamma' means the literary corpus of canonical teaching. . . . The word 'pada' means support." As suggested earlier, therefore, some such title as "The Sayings of the Master" would, without doing unforgivable violence to the original, cover the sayings of Moses in the Book of Deuteronomy, the sayings of Jesus in the Four Gospels, the sayings of Muhammad in the Qur'ān, the sayings of Confucius in the Analects, and the sayings of Gotama Buddha here in the Dhammapada.

Composition and Authorship. The foundation of Buddhism was not written but oral, in the preaching of Gotama Buddha during the sixth century B.C.E.; more precise dating than this seems difficult to achieve. The Dhammapada appears to be referring to this preaching when it speaks of "a well-spoken word fruitful for one who does it" (52); as the commentary on this passage explains, "the 'well-spoken word' means the Word of the Buddha contained in the three *pitakas.*" Already during his lifetime, the sayings of Gotama were being memorized and repeated by his disciples. These have survived in many versions and recensions, of which the Dhammapada is one of the most widely received. Such versions of the teachings of Gotama, often introduced with the formula "Thus have I heard," inextricably combine authentic original sayings with the development of later tradition. They differ widely not only in their content but in their literary form. A large number of them are in prose, cast in the form of a discourse by the Master and an acknowledgment by the hearer. The sayings in the Dhammapada, however, are arranged in verse structure, whether or not they were in fact spoken that way originally, at least partly as a mnemonic device and as a basis for ritual recitation. Reducing all of this oral tradition to written form must have taken several centuries after the life of Gotama Buddha, and stabilizing the written versions of the many components of Buddhist scripture into a "canon," or actually into several canons, took even longer (see "Canon" below). In the case of the material in the Dhammapada, the codification and circulation of the work resulted in its wide circulation and broad acceptance, and various individual verses have parallels and echoes throughout Buddhist literature of sayings attributed to the Buddha. As Carter and Palihawadana point out in their introduction, besides this Pali version to which the specific title "Dhammapada" applies, "other Buddhist schools that originated in India also seem to have had their own versions of this text, of which only three are extant at the present time—the *Udānavarga* in Sanskrit, the *Gāndhārī Dharmapada* in Prakrit, and the recently published text known as the *Patna Dharmapada*, which is in a language close to Pali." In addition, Max Müller claimed to have knowledge of translations of the Dhammapada, or at any rate of a work that significantly overlaps with the Dhammapada, in Chinese and in Tibetan.

Language and Text. Some of the earliest oral accounts and written deposits of the teachings of Gotama Buddha were in Sanskrit, but the language of the Dhammapada, as well as of all the other works in the canon of Theravāda Buddhism, is Pali, which bears a strong linguistic connection to Sanskrit and Vedic (see chapter 5). The various vernacular languages seemed to Gotama himself to be preferable to Sanskrit, the language of the scholars and sages. Nevertheless, Pali itself eventually became a scholar's language, and it is studied today by those, in East or West, who want to understand the Buddhist tradition in its oldest written form. The Pali Dhammapada came into being in Sri Lanka, into which Buddhism spread in the third century B.C.E., first in the form of the oral tradition; and from Sri Lanka, eventually in written form, the Dhammapada was carried to most of Southeast Asia, where it is revered and studied to this day. Having been originated and transmitted orally, the text of the Dhammapada has repeatedly proved baffling to its editors and translators. The production of the first edition of the original Pali text in accordance with critical philological standards, based on three Pali manuscripts with a Latin translation, was the work of a Danish scholar, V. Fausbøll, in 1855; a second edition appeared in 1900. Max Müller pays it the compliment of declaring that "there was no other scholar living at the time who would have ventured on such new ground as that chosen by the young Danish scholar." Philological work on the Dhammapada has continued since Fausbøll's edition. Nevertheless, for a number of passages in the present edition, the translators, having consulted all the available materials, have been obliged to confess that "even the combined benefit of the study of these sources could not always give us the enlightenment that we would have desired on some intricacies of our text and its commentary. In some cases at least, this could conceivably be due to 'corruption' in the process of transmission of the text in Sri Lanka." Even after all their research, moreover, they have found that "too many problems remain, and indeed some of the problems connected with the text are likely to remain unsolved, though it is to be hoped that future research may reduce their number."

Canon and Authority. Nowhere in these *Sacred Writings* is the problem of canon and authority more acute and more complicated than in the study of Buddhism. Just as Judaism and the major confessional divisions of Christianity are defined in part by the disagreements about which books should and should not be included in the biblical canon (see chapters 1 and 2), so the three divisions of Buddhism—Theravāda ("Way of the Elders") or Hīnayāna ("Lesser Vehicle"), Mahāyāna ("Greater Vehicle"), and Mantrayāna or Vajrayāna—have divergent canons. The sheer mass of the total Buddhist corpus of Sacred Books, even in the Hīnayāna Pali canon alone, is overwhelming. The Pali canon comprises thirty-two books in all, collected in "the Three Baskets" or Tipitaka: the Vinaya-Pitaka, "Basket of Discipline," which is a compilation intended chiefly or even exclusively for Buddhist monks; the Sutta-Pitaka, "Basket of

Discourses," in which Buddhist doctrine is expounded in the form of discourses by the Buddha; and the Abhidhamma-Pitaka, a title translated by some Western students as "Basket of Scholasticism," which deals with questions of metaphysics. The Dhammapada belongs to the second of the Three Baskets and holds a position of honor within Buddhist spirituality. More than most of the other books in the Pali canon or in the canons of the other Buddhist groups, it can lay claim to an "ecumenical" authority, which was, indeed, one of the most important considerations in its being chosen for inclusion here; for in content if not in form, the maxims and precepts it attributes to the teachings of Gotama Buddha are, by and large, the common property of all those who profess to be his disciples.

Traditional Interpretation. The text of the present edition of the Dhammapada, unlike that of the other Sacred Books in this set, includes as an integral part of the work an early quasi-canonical commentary, as well as a transliteration of the Pali text of the Dhammapada. The reason for including the commentary is its wealth of indispensable explanatory glosses on words and concepts of the Dhammapada that might otherwise be totally obscure. It was on that basis that Carter and Palihawadana decided "to combine the translation of the verses of the *Dhammapada* with the expository text that immediately follows them in the traditional commentary (which is now extant only in the Pali translation made of it some time after the fifth century A.D.), and to supplement this with notes drawn from some of the major interpretive works on the *Dhammapada* written in Sri Lanka." Within the tradition of Western scholarly interpretation of the Buddhist scriptures, the Dhammapada has likewise come to occupy an important place because of its relative transparency and accessibility.

Translations and This Translation. The history of the successive translations of the Dhammapada into Western languages is an epitome of the gradual discovery of Buddhism by scholars and thinkers.

Fausbøll's Latin translation, followed by Max Müller's English translation, opened the work to Western readers. The Pali Text Society, as part of its series of "Sacred Books of the Buddhists," published the Dhammapada in 1931. Because of his eminence as a philosopher-statesman and as the author of the widely influential *Eastern Religions and Western Thought* (2d ed., 1940), Sarvepalli Radhakrishnan's edition of the Pali text and English translation with notes, published in 1950, has been warmly received. The translation we are presenting here, the joint labor of John Ross Carter and Mahinda Palihawadana, is the result of a special, if not quite unique, collaboration between Eastern and Western scholarship and, as they put it, of a "long-distance correspondence between Hamilton, New York, and Maharagama, Sri Lanka."

II

METHODS OF STUDY

7

THE PEOPLE OF THE BOOK

Religion has been defined, in the celebrated formulation of the American philosopher William James, as "the feelings, acts, and experiences of individual men in their solitude, so far as they apprehend themselves to stand in relation to whatever they may consider the divine"; another Harvard professor, Alfred North Whitehead, defined it as "what the individual does with his own solitariness." Now it is a teaching shared by many religions and urged by many sacred books that "the kingdom of God is within you" (Luke 17:21 AV), even though there have also been some religions—including, according to many historians, the official religion of ancient Rome—that have stressed outward observance almost to the exclusion of private spirituality. As we shall have occasion to note more than once, the practice of private devotion, and of mystical contemplation, does act as an important resource for reading and understanding any sacred book. Nevertheless, just as it is at best one-sided and at worst distorted to define religion exclusively on the basis of the solitary individual, so it is, if anything, even more important for the understanding of the

Sacred Book than it is for mystical devotion to locate it within the community of faith and its tradition.

The reason for this importance is that in each case it is the community of faith that has written the Sacred Book or, at the very least, has acknowledged the Book as sacred. And, looking at the question from the opposite direction, it is by means of the Sacred Book, or sometimes by means of a particular interpretation of the Sacred Book, that the community of faith has defined itself. "The People of the Book" is a Muslim term, used in the Qur'ān (e.g., 3:64–66) and applied now to the three "book monotheisms" claiming Abraham as their father: following the usual Muslim order, Islam, Judaism, and Christianity. But by extension the name may legitimately be applied to any sacred community that lives by a sacred book. To begin with, the Sacred Book is often the emblem by which a community of faith sets itself apart—or, in the literal etymology of the word, "de-fines" itself, by fixing the boundaries—in relation to other communities. Rudyard Kipling's phrase "lesser breeds without the Law" was surely Euro-centric and probably racist, but it was only his version of such de-fining on the basis of "the Law" that "we" have and "they" presumably do not. That self-definition of the community has, in both subtle and overt ways, affected the Sacred Book itself, helping to determine what should be in and what should be out, and a judicious reader of the Book will be on the lookout for evidence of this process as part of the key to understanding.

For the Sacred Book is a key to the history of the people, and the history of the people is a key to the Sacred Book. This mutuality implies that the sacred history the Book narrates and the sacred history the people of the Book have experienced interpenetrate each other at all levels. Even in phrases and stories of the Sacred Book that do not refer to the history outright, the history continues to be present, so that ignoring it can lead to grave misunderstanding. When we as readers of a sacred book come upon the use of the singular somewhere—for example, the name "Adam" in the Tanakh, the New Testament, and the Qur'ān—that does not necessarily imply that reference is to an individual apart from the community. Indeed, it may often imply the very opposite, that the community itself—in the case of Adam, the community of the entire human race—is speaking. In other instances it implies that the individual is functioning here as a representative and spokesman for the community, or as a representative and spokesman of the Holy toward the community, perhaps even against it. Sometimes, as in the case of the Tanakh, the communal history covered by the Sacred Book itself extends over several millennia, and sometimes, as in the case of the New Testament, it is no more than a century or so. Trying to identify the locus of an incident or a saying within the history will often help to give it meaning. The very figures of speech in which a people of the Book will strive to come to terms with some later event spring to mind almost unconsciously from the sacred page: an indelible example from our own time is Holocaust, the term used in the Septuagint Greek translation of such passages as Leviticus 6 in the Tanakh for what our version calls "the ritual of the burnt offering."

A people of the Book may or may not think of itself as unique, but it cannot evade—and neither can the present-day reader of the Book—the question of its relation as a community of faith and observance to other communities. Much of what a sacred book describes or prescribes, for example, pertains to a much smaller community than the people as a whole, notably to the family. The home is the place where many first encounter the Sacred Book, as part of growing up and as an accompaniment to the rites of passage through life, from birth to schooling to marriage to the grave. Even readers who are not attempting to conform their lives to the standards set down in the Sacred Book should always be attentive to the communities and sub-communities to which and for which it speaks. Conversely, because of the role of the Sacred Book in identifying the people of the Book, there is always a political dimension present, even when it is not overt. The story of Moses standing before Pharaoh, demanding in the name of the Lord "Let my people go!" (Ex. 9:1) may apply, by metaphor or allegory, to the liberation of the individual soul from the bonds of sin or from a demonic addiction; it *must* apply to the deliverance of an entire people from bondage, whether by the Exodus or by the Emancipation Proclamation. The history of religious-political fanaticism and of the idea of "holy war" in our own time has demonstrated yet again that the theocratic ideal of an equation of the political entity (or, in modern terms, the state) with the people of the Book is always a possibility—and often a danger. How the natural ties of family or ethnicity fit in with the definition of the people of the Book is an issue that the reader of a sacred book must continually recognize, as Abraham Lincoln did when he spoke of the United States as "the almost chosen people."

Closely related to this political dimension, but distinct enough to warrant special mention as a key for reading a sacred book, is the place of legislation within its covers, to which we shall return in a later chapter. The very name Torah, which originally means simply "teaching," has come to acquire the specific meaning "law," and each of the six Sacred Books in this set contains some rules and regulations. Some of these are very individualistic and strictly "private," dealing with some of the most intimate of human experiences. Yet even these belong to the ground rules by which the community as people of the Book orders the common life, as the regulations governing the ritual bath and circumcision show. Whenever one reads a sacred book belonging to another tradition, one is inevitably struck by minute prohibitions or prescriptions that to an outsider must seem quite esoteric or even trivial. Indeed, when one returns to portions of one's own Sacred Book after some interval, there are always exotic details about proper clothing or ritual purification that do not seem to have been there before, and their purpose, for heaven or even for earth, seems utterly impenetrable. Yet even for interpreting these, the social setting of private rules and sayings within the sacred community can be a useful key. That applies all the more, it seems, to the legislation of the Book for the people as a whole. As we shall have opportunity to note again later, virtually every religion has feasts and fasts and festivals, sacred times and sacred places, that are set aside for the Holy. Regulating these, standardizing their observance without stifling the creative urges of individual piety, and keeping potentially dangerous extravagances within bounds is the function of the religious jurisprudence by which the Sacred Book helps to give the people of the Book its historical identity.

That identity, moreover, is not exhausted by the history that is contained in the Book, and an essential focus for understanding the Book and its people is holy tradition. Both by explicit cross-references and by tacit acknowledgments, the Sacred Book points back to the tradition out of which it has come. These cross-references and tacit acknowledgments are not always easy to pick up, but an alert reader can sometimes tease them out of the text by constantly pondering what kinds of collective experience and tradition seem to underlie it: does the story of the binding of Isaac in Genesis 22 mean that there was a Near Eastern tradition of child sacrifice with which Israel had to deal? Are the recitations of the story of the Exodus from Egypt part of a liturgical tradition, an annual ritual of "owning the Covenant," even though the materials in the Torah on the Passover observance fail to include this and other features that have been incorporated into the later observance of the commemoration of the Exodus, as this is prescribed in the ceremonies of the Haggadah? Sometimes the reason that some part of an earlier tradition has not been included in the Sacred Book is itself an interesting speculative question, although the historical resources for answering that question may be extremely limited. Such limitations have, to be sure, never kept students of Sacred Books from either asking or answering such questions. In many cases, earlier traditions that were not included in the Sacred Book, for whatever reason, have nevertheless persisted and have become parts of the "postbiblical" tradition, even though they are actually "prebiblical" in their origins.

And "postbiblical" often, though not always, may also mean less authoritative. Thus in every people of the Book there is some version of the debate between the primal authority of the sacred text and the later authority of the accumulated—and still accumulating—tradition. The reformers who have arisen within the peoples of the Book may sometimes lay claim to a new insight or revelation that supersedes the older ones, including those in the Sacred Book itself, but more often such new insight presents itself in the form of a deeper understanding intended by the holy writer or by the Holy that was the writer's inspiration. There is tradition in every religion, in fact in every society whether primitive or modern, but it is characteristic of religions of the Book that the tradition is in many fundamental ways a tradition of exegesis. If a reader, whether a member of that people of the Book or not, wants to read and understand the Sacred Book, it is presumptuous to act as though no one had ever read or understood it before. This resource is distinct, though not completely separate, from the critical scholarly traditions that also adhere to the text, but simple courtesy as well as historical sensitivity would seem to require that before I pull rabbits out of a hat on my own or learn the most recent theories of some professor somewhere, I should try to see the Sacred Book in the life and history of its own people, giving them the first voice to which I listen. Gilbert K. Chesterton once defined tradition as "extending the franchise to our ancestors," and this would seem to be the right way to treat other people's ancestors, too, when we study a sacred book that belongs to them.

There is one important respect in which no reader inside or outside the community can forget that the Sacred Book does belong to the people of the Book past and present, and that is in the determination of the very table of contents of the Book. In the case of a sacred book the usual term for table of contents is "canon," which means "norm"; each of the six introductory chapters here includes a paragraph under that title. What I hold in my hand when I pick up each of these Sacred Books is the result of a process by which someone back there somewhere decided that this particular collection of writings would constitute the norm or rule for believing, living, and praying, hence the "canon." The fecundity of religious experience in spawning hymns and poems, affirmations and doxologies, is notorious, and so is the propensity of religious establishments for censoring those expressions deemed to be aberrations, while elevating to canonical status those that seem to merit such a status. Thus a short time after the death of Gotama Buddha, a council was held at Rajagaha which began the process of fixing the "Pali Canon" of Buddhist Scripture (see chapter 6); and at Jamnia, some time after the Roman sack of Jerusalem in 70 C.E., there was, according to some scholars, a Jewish council to discuss the canonicity of certain books. Even those Sacred Books that have resulted from a single set of experiences and revelations, like the ones that came to the Prophet Muhammad to form the Qur'ān, have not completely escaped the controversy over canon. But such controversy has been particularly virulent in those groups where the question of canon has arisen after the fact, when the accumulations of the centuries do finally have to be sorted out by separating the authentic from the inauthentic or the less authentic, the wheat from the chaff. Such a process of sorting, and by whatever criteria, may take a long time, and even after such a time it is often anything but final. In principle the ideal may be a single norm, but historically the norms—and the canons of the Sacred Book—are pluralistic.

All along I have been using the term "people of the Book" in the singular, as though there were one people for each Book and one Book for each people, when in fact the same Sacred Book, in whole or in part, may carry normative force for more than one people—and "one people" may not really be one at all. For a force that claims to unite humanity with God and thus in God to unite humanity itself, religion has displayed an astonishing capacity to divide not only the adherents of one faith from the adherents of another but some adherents of one faith from other adherents of the same faith—and thus some readers of a sacred book from other readers of the same sacred book. It would not be fair to inflict on every reader of every Sacred Book a catalog of the schisms, sects, and controversies that have come from encounters with the same normative Book. But endless confusion can result, even at a purely external level, if a reader does not realize, for example, that the Qur'ān and the Rig Veda have been arranged differently in different versions, that different groups count the Psalms differently, and that even the Ten Commandments are not numbered the same way in all denominations. Far graver are the consequences of sectarianism and schism over the basic meaning of the Sacred Book itself. To call the Tanakh by its Christian designation "the Old Testament" is, without even having to say it, to posit the existence of a Testament that is "New," which continues/supplements/supersedes the Old. Even a reader who is determined to travel light and to avoid excess baggage does have to carry some of this information about what by this time we should probably be calling "the peoples of the Books."

8

THE COMMUNITY OF
SCRIBES AND SCHOLARS

It seems safe to guess that during the past two or three centuries more
scholars have lavished more care on these Sacred Books than on any
comparable number of words and pages in the world—on some, to be
sure, more than on others, and probably more on the New Testament
than on all the others combined, but also in amazing detail on each of
these Sacred Books. As a result, if an unsuspecting reader of these
Sacred Writings decides to drop into the local library just to check out a
few titles, the result will be a deluge of catalog entries: critical editions
of the original text and annotated translations into various languages,
scholarly monographs and learned journals, proceedings of international conferences and countless Ph.D. dissertations, all with no end in
sight. The only possible response is the sigh of King Solomon, "The
making of many books is without limit, and much study is a wearying
of the flesh" (Eccles. 12:12)—or perhaps the classic thank-you letter of
the child, "Dear Auntie, The book told me more about penguins than
I ever wanted to know!" For thousands of years and in many religions
and cultures, the spectacle of quarrels among the learned over minutiae

of the text while the people are starving for spiritual food has been a recurring theme for reformers and satirists, and with good reason. When, as has periodically been the case and especially during recent centuries, the scholars have at the same time been neutral or even hostile to the text and the tradition, seemingly employing the methods of critical research to undermine the faith, the negative reaction to their work sounds a correspondingly polemical note.

Therefore the first observation to be made about the scholarly study of the Sacred Books is the reminder that by no means have all of the scholars who worked on them been hostile. In fact, the hostile modern scholars would not have had texts to study and criticize if there had not been devout and patient scribes and grammarians over many centuries who faithfully transmitted the sacred text to later generations. While it simply is not true, as is often said these days in the heat of debate, that it is impossible for an outsider to understand Christian or Jewish or Buddhist (or black or female or, for that matter, Slavic) writings or that only a believer has the right to explain a sacred book—a position that would make Egyptian hieroglyphics, Homeric religion, or Druidism totally inaccessible to anyone today—it is true that the believing scholars of past and present always have much to contribute to our understanding of a sacred book. In the case of some of these Sacred Books, for example the Qur'ān or the Rig Veda, the research of Western scholars from outside the community of faith—some of them now being reprinted in the lands, such as Egypt and India, where these Sacred Books are normative—has acted in modern times as a catalyst to stimulate the historical and philological work of those scholars who adhere to this Sacred Book as a standard for life and faith. Increasingly, moreover, the publications of such scholars from Asia and Africa are appearing in English and other Western languages, adding to the card catalogs but also to the clarification of the Sacred Books. For such scholarship, too, the Sacred Book is not merely something out of a museum, but part of the total culture of a people of the Book, to be studied with the same affectionate feeling and close attention that one gives to a letter from one's beloved, for to the eyes of faith that is really what it is.

Even those readers within a community of faith will have to acknowledge, however, the massive contribution that has come to the understanding of their Sacred Book above all from the critical historical and literary scholarship of investigators who are not by any definition orthodox believers. Despite a grateful recognition of the patient work of the scribes in the various scriptoria East and West in passing on the sacred manuscripts, no one can be blind to the massive textual problems that still remain in each of these Sacred Books. There are obvious misspellings or mistakes, made many centuries and many manuscripts ago and perpetuated precisely because the scribes have been so faithful. Where the scribes had to choose from among the variant readings they encountered, they were often naive and sometimes arbitrary, mechanically counting manuscripts pro and con even when most of the manuscripts were derived from one manuscript and should therefore have been counted together for only one vote. Textual criticism, whether applied to a sacred book or to the folios of Shakespeare, remains something less than an exact science, but it is a science as well as an art and it can go a long way toward determining the degrees of probability for different readings. It should perhaps be added that the textual criticism of the folios of Shakespeare or of the manuscripts of James Joyce proceeds in considerable measure by the methods and rules modern scholars of Sacred Books have worked out. Discriminating readers will want to be thankfully aware that the renderings of the texts of the Sacred Books included in this set reflect the application of that art and science of textual criticism, and it is a tribute to the increasing sophistication of such readers, as well as to that of translators, editors, and publishers, that recent editions of various Sacred Books have been incorporating information about this so-called "lower criticism" in their footnotes and critical apparatus.

Unavoidably, such scholarly information is often rather arcane, and there are some who find it disturbing to know that the sacred text may not be absolutely reliable in every letter. But the importance of textual criticism as a tool for reading the Sacred Books is more than equaled—and its capacity to disturb is exceeded—by the "higher criticism" of Sacred Books, which deals with such questions as authorship. As each of our introductory chapters has suggested, the derivation of Sacred Books from tradition implies that the process of reducing the tradition to its final written form may have taken considerable time and may have involved multiple sources. The eighteenth century saw the rise of the "documentary hypothesis" as a method of literary history, applicable to the poems of Homer (whoever he or they may have been) as well as to Sacred Books, with somewhat similar results in the identification of such supposed sources. Although the study of Homer no less than the study of Sacred Books during the twentieth century has come to place greater emphasis on the oral transmission of the materials that eventually became the text, rather than on alleged written documents that were stitched together by some unknown redactor, one underlying scholarly presupposition remains the same: in studying a sacred book, whether one's own or someone else's, it is appropriate and justifiable to apply the same methods of historical-literary analysis that students of other, less hallowed ancient texts employ. The outcome of such analysis, however, is often at variance with the received views within the community of faith about the composition of the book. A reader will want to learn at least something about current scholarly theories of the authorship and origin of a sacred book, but should also learn how to take the book as it stands, whatever its historical or prehistorical development may have been, and to read it as an artifact in its own right. For it is characteristic of every Sacred Book that it speaks with an immediacy and directness over which—as even a scholar is sometimes tempted to say, "Thank God!"—the scholars have little control.

Almost certainly the most valuable contribution of scholarship to the general reader is in the study of the immediate historical context of these Sacred Books. It is part of the "paradox of understanding" discussed earlier that the work of the historical scholars on this context has illumined the world of thought reflected in the Sacred Book and at the same time has made it even stranger than it was before. A twentieth-century Western mind trying to encompass the Analects of Confucius can derive great benefit from the sympathetic and learned treatment by Benjamin Schwartz in his book *The World of Thought in Ancient China*. Many of the individual sayings in the Analects, but also the style of teaching and learning that the Analects presuppose, become far clearer than they would be if one simply picked up the book cold and started to read it. At the same time, unfortunately, some passages in each of these Sacred Books that seem, at least in some translations, to speak directly to the needs and state of mind of any serious person become more obscure intellectually—and, at least at first, less accessible religiously—in the light of the historical context: the saying of Jesus, "Whoever endures to the end will be saved" (Matt. 10:22), does not really mean, as countless sermons have suggested, that the relation of the individual with God is "till death do us part," but, as the context shows, that this world is about to come to an end. Yet there is no justification for a Luddite reaction to historical scholarship, even from readers with a propensity for the allegorical interpretation of a sacred book. It is a long-established principle of allegory that although the literal meaning of the text may be misleading, it remains the most reliable place to start; for us in the twentieth century the literal meaning of any text must be the one that comes not only from grammatical or literary analysis, but also from historical research.

It is chiefly from the study of the historical context of Sacred Books that we learn to understand in depth the variety of literary forms present in them—an issue to which we shall return later. As attention to those literary forms indicates, a major resource for the scholarly study of Sacred Books has been the comparative method. It is often a corollary of religious loyalty to believe in the distinctiveness, indeed the uniqueness, of "our" Sacred Book, and to dismiss as relativism— or as heresy or blasphemy—any effort to find analogies and parallels for it in any other Sacred Books. But when such parallels truly are too obvious to be dismissed, the alternative strategy is to attribute originality to ours and plagiarism to theirs, even when the chronological facts make this extremely implausible. Despite such defensiveness, however, the comparative method of scholars during the past century or two has been overwhelmingly positive in its results. When the dazzling visions and the transcendent message of the angel Gabriel to Muhammad take their place among the revelations to other prophets in other traditions—with at least some of whom, such as Moses and Jesus, the Prophet Muhammad proudly claimed affinity in the very pages of the Qur'ān (7:103–62, 3:45–59)—they are illumined in various ways. To the predominantly literary preoccupations of earlier comparativists more recent scholars have added insights from anthropology, folklore, and even psychoanalysis, with results that may often have been controversial and may sometimes have been silly, but that have also sometimes provoked many readers of Sacred Books to look at familiar materials from a fresh perspective. It is only necessary to mention Mircea Eliade's application of ideas from anthropology and from Jungian psychology to the myths of creation in various religions to suggest the riches of insight that such comparative-historical scholarship brings to any reader of Sacred Books, believer or not.

But once we have enlarged the community of scholars to include not merely scribes, exegetes, talmudists, theologians, and philosophers, but literary scholars, cultural historians, and social scientists, we are no longer within the circle of faith, and we are obliged to admit that readers of Sacred Books have much to learn from such "secular" scholars. It says a great deal about the realities of religious faith and religious prejudice that almost all readers would be prepared to admit that about all other Sacred Books than their own! Yet it is the all but universal testimony of representative believers from each of the six traditions represented here in *Sacred Writings* that they have come away from their study of the works of comparative scholars deepened and strengthened in their understanding and appreciation of their own Sacred Book, even as those scholars have likewise helped them to make the acquaintance of other Sacred Books they had thought of as utterly alien. This is an experience we hope may be duplicated also by some of the readers of these *Sacred Writings*.

9

THE SACRED LANGUAGE

Although most readers of this set will come to it with English as their first language, or even as their only language, they need to realize the obvious and yet not so obvious fact that all six of these Sacred Books are translations from some ancient original language: in order of appearance, Hebrew (plus a little Aramaic), Greek, Arabic, Chinese, Sanskrit, and Pali. "Translators are traitors," an Italian proverb says, confirming the disappointment that is experienced over and over by native speakers of any language whenever the rendering of a work into a second language fails to do justice to the original—as, by definition, it always does. There is much to be said in favor of the nineteenth-century Romantic notion that a nation's language is the one indispensable key to its authentic genius and to the spirit of its deepest traditions. "The German language," wrote the poet Friedrich Klopstock, "is the way we once were: unique." Even people who are ignorant of other languages, as speakers of English all too often tend to be, ought to recognize that only a rank beginner in the study of another language, and only an extremely naive reader of any translation, will suppose that there is some sort of one-to-one equivalency between any two languages, as though the same term in Sanskrit or Hebrew (or Russian or Japanese) could always be uniformly Englished. The history of international diplomacy is replete with anecdotes about misunderstandings, which would be funny if they were not so serious, that have been generated by somebody's failure to grasp the intended nuance in a communication between governments, simply because the translation could not, or at any rate did not, do it justice. Less grave and therefore more comic are the many stories about how immigrants, and even the children and grandchildren of immigrants, missed the insulting or vulgar overtones of a word or phrase when they were thinking in one language but speaking or writing in another. For it is, as often as not, the connotations of an idiomatic expression in one language that fail to find their way into the other. That problem afflicts even the supposedly objective languages of science and engineering or of international finance, as we are beginning to learn now that the whole world is becoming a single market.

Nor is the difficulty of achieving fidelity in a translation simply a function of knowing the vocabulary and finding the right words. Even between languages that belong to the same family, there are deep and subtle differences in syntax. The differences are deeper and subtler between languages that stand in a completely alien tradition, which for speakers of English is the case with all the languages in which these Sacred Books were originally written, except, in a remote way, Sanskrit and Greek. Arabic and Hebrew, for example, will frequently dispense with forms of the verb "to be" where English and other Western languages seem to require one: "This *is* the day that the Lord has made" (Ps. 118:24). But sometimes it is "to signify" rather than "to be" that the text implies rather than says, as when Joseph tells Pharaoh, "The seven healthy cows *are* seven years" (Gen. 41:26). Even between English and Greek, which is the closest to English of all the languages represented here, a reader should be aware of these subtle but profound differences of syntax. It would be highly intrusive for the translators of any of these Sacred Books to call attention each time to instances of such modulation of key across languages, but "truth in packaging" would seem to require that readers who cannot check the original receive the warning that something like this has been going on.

All these problems of translating are compounded when the original is poetry. Should opera be sung in the original, as it usually is in the United States, or in the language of the audience, as it often is in Europe? In part the answer to that question is rooted in this general problem. "It is a pretty poem, Mr. Pope," Richard Bentley said when Alexander Pope published his version of the *Iliad* in 1715, "but you must not call it Homer!" And it was not Homer, but at least it was a "pretty poem," and that is rather more than can be said for some English versions of Greek epic, which are so pedantic and two-dimensional that the English reader cannot get any understanding from them at all of why these epics have been gripping the human heart for more than twenty-five centuries. Among poems, moreover, it is above all lyric poetry that makes translators into traitors: the compact form of the lyric does not leave room for translators to establish a pattern or to find their voice, because by the time they have begun to do so the poem is over. Americans and West Europeans always have great difficulty understanding why so many Russians put Pushkin in the first place among authors in their language, above even Dostoevsky and Tolstoy; this discrepancy, while complex in its origins, appears to be due at least in part to the difficulty of finding a voice in English for the poetry of Pushkin. Yet the qualitative difference between prose and poetry as a subject for translation becomes infinitely more complicated still when a translator undertakes, as have the various scholars and authors whose work has gone into this set, to carry over into another language and another culture the deepest expressions of the spirituality of a people as it is documented in its

Sacred Books. Anyone who has ever attempted it, even as a student exercise, will confess to having known their anguish firsthand.

That situation makes it understandable when the devotees of some Sacred Books have despaired of the effort, arguing that if the Holy has chosen to reveal Itself through the medium of a particular language, it is incumbent upon the faithful to learn that language in order to read that Sacred Book. The most fully articulated enshrinement of the sacred language as the indispensable key to the Sacred Book is probably the Muslim reverence for Arabic as the original language of the Qur'ān. The distinguished modern Muslim scholar Muhammad Abduh speaks of how "foreign converts to Islam came to appreciate the imperative need to retain the integrity of the Arabic language." Statistically, the number of non-Arabic Muslims in a world Islamic population of about a billion is greater than that of Arab adherents, for whom the sacred language is a native tongue, or at any rate the ancestor of their native tongue. In Iran or Pakistan or Kazakhstan, the close connection between the Qur'ān and its original language has often been a hardship for those who aspire to deeper knowledge of the faith or to a clerical career. Nevertheless, our translation of the Qur'ān by the Pakistani poet Ahmed Ali is evidence of how profoundly and sensitively a non-Arab is able to grasp the sacred text and, having grasped it, to render it into an altogether different tongue, indeed into a tongue that is also different from his own native language (which is Urdu).

This bilingual edition of his translation of the Qur'ān also illustrates one of the most splendid by-products that can come from the reverence for the original language. Combined as it is with the resistance to any idolatry, such reverence led Islamic culture to a cultivation of the art of writing the sacred tongue of the Qur'ān in a calligraphy that has only rarely been matched in the history of human literacy. Although the Qur'ān is a special case of the primacy of the sacred language for the understanding of the Sacred Book, it is by no means the only example. Our edition of the Dhammapada not only translates the Pali text, but transliterates it. The translation of the Hebrew Bible into Greek by the Hellenistic Jews of Alexandria from the third to the first centuries B.C.E., the so-called Septuagint, was used by Christians for their own purposes in such a way that dissuaded the adherents of Judaism from the very idea of translating the Torah again. It rendered the Hebrew word in Isaiah 7:14, translated "young woman" in our version of the Tanakh, with "virgin," which the New Testament was able to quote in support of Christian teaching (Matt. 1:22–23). Therefore when the dominant literary language of parts of the Mediterranean world became Latin once more in the third and fourth centuries C.E., it was the Christians through the Vulgate, not the Jews through a Latin translation of the Tanakh, who made the Bible known to the Gentiles. Similarly, the translations of the Buddhist Sacred Books into Chinese are still regarded with admiration by scholars of both Buddhism and Chinese, who also, however, point to the subtle but profound differences that took place in Buddhist doctrine as a consequence. In the words of a distinguished scholar of Chinese Buddhism, Arthur Wright, "Everyone who has contemplated the process by which Indian ideas and institutions were made intelligible and, to a degree, acceptable to the Chinese has been struck by the breadth of the cultural gulf which had to be overcome."

Formidable as these attendant difficulties undoubtedly are, they have, obviously, not managed to deter translators from the attempt to make Sacred Books speak in other tongues, as the six volumes of this set demonstrate. Because of the inner impulse to share the faith with others, which believers belonging to many traditions accept as a divine imperative, there has certainly been more translating of Sacred Books—and over a longer period of time—than of any other writings in the whole history of literature. It is to this enterprise of translation that many peoples have owed the first reduction of their vernacular languages to written form and hence also the very creation of their alphabet, as when Cyril and Methodius came to the Slavs in the ninth century. That process has been continuing throughout the world even during the twentieth century, chiefly through the work of Christian missionaries. The reader of any Sacred Book must also keep in mind the widespread propensity of religious faith for identifying archaic language, sometimes even the archaic language of an early translation, as the sacred language. The story of the pious soul who believed that the most sacred word in the English language was (spoken slowly) "Me-so-po-ta-mi-a" may be a fiction, but the old-fashioned English pronoun "thou" has lived on in the language of love ("How can I leave thee? How can I from thee part?") and in the language of patriotism ("My country, 'tis of thee"), but above all in the language of religious faith, together with the "plain speech" of those groups such as the Society of Friends who pattern their English usage after it. No one speaks the classical Arabic of the Qur'ān today, and Sanskrit is studied only by those who want to understand the Sacred Books of Hinduism and by those scholars in linguistics who want to examine the historic roots of modern Indo-European languages. In the period of the New Testament, the Hebrew of the Tanakh had fallen into disuse among Jews even in Palestine, and Jesus and his disciples spoke Aramaic; it was only in modern times that Hebrew was revived, becoming the vernacular of the state of Israel. The Authorized ("King James") Version of the Bible and the plays of Shakespeare have immortalized Elizabethan English for succeeding generations. Thus the very quaintness of the forms of speech in a sacred book, whether in the original or in a classic translation, somehow seems to lend enchantment and to evoke reverence, and resistance to changes in those forms of speech has often provoked controversy, and even schism, down to the twentieth century.

It is not simply an easy way out of the dilemma of the translator as traitor when each of the translations included here sometimes resorts to transliterating or adapting certain terms and titles from the sacred language instead of attempting to find or to coin an English equivalent. "Analects" is such an equivalent, and "Bible" is a Graeco-Latin word (originally meaning "books," in the plural) for the Hebrew collection of Sacred Books. But the Hebrew "Tanakh," and above all the Arabic "Qur'ān" and the Sanskrit "Veda" now have a rightful place in English and other languages, for which "The Recitation" or "The Knowledge" would not be an acceptable substitute. Every faith and every Sacred Book would seem to have a right to a certain number of such sacred loan words. Once they have come into the new language as part of a translation, these words may eventually find a permanent home, so that we can speak of "Nirvana" (rendered as "Nibbāna" in the translation of the Dhammapada by John Ross Carter and Mahinda Palihawadana being used here) or "Sabbath" almost as common nouns to be spelled with lower-case initials and to be applied to secular life, and can say "Amen" at the end of a petition regardless of the name of the deity—if any—to whom that petition is addressed. There is a fine line between abdicating the translator's responsibility by dotting the page with one transliterated loan word after another, until the poor reader has to know the original to understand the translation, and laying violent Eurocentric hands on an ancient and venerable text by superimposing Judaeo-Christian vocabulary on it, as has often been done, for example, even in the translations of Plato into English and other modern European languages. The learned may quarrel with the translations in this set for having crossed that fine line in one direction or the other or both, but there seems to be a consensus among most fair-minded critics that each of the translations has struck a reasonable balance between the extremes.

At a time when the realities of transportation, communication, and commerce are bringing the peoples of the world into ever closer contact, if not into ever closer harmony, it may be permissible to express the hope that the need to understand the spirituality of others will provide some added incentive for the increased study of foreign languages, ancient as well as modern, including the original Hebrew, Greek, Arabic, Chinese, Sanskrit, and Pali of these six Sacred Books. For there is a sense in which it is true that if a translation is to achieve its purpose, it must at one and the same time be clear enough in its renderings to convey the content of the original and be unclear enough to remind the reader that it is not the original; that, too, belongs to the paradox of understanding. Therefore the reader ought to keep in mind that when Confucius in the Analects speaks of "Heaven" or Muhammad in the Qur'ān of "Allah," this is—and yet it is not—what a Western reader with a Jewish or Christian background may mean by "God," and that this paradox, too, is an expression of the Ultimate Mystery for which none of these names is sufficient. As believers of all traditions have acknowledged, we use such names not in order to say something specific about the real nature of the Holy, but in order not to have to remain altogether silent.

10

THE FOUNDER-SAGE

The conviction that there is no God except Allah and that Muhammad is the Prophet of Allah is the fundamental creed of the Islamic faith and the central message of its Sacred Book, the Qur'ān. Not every religion has such a "founder," whether historical or mythical, and ultimately every religion claims to have been founded by none other than the Holy Itself. Yet it is a special characteristic of those religions that do have a sacred book that many of them look to the authority of some historical person to whom and through whom the Holy has spoken and acted in a decisive fashion. Indeed, of the six world religions represented in this set of *Sacred Writings*, only the Hinduism of the Rig Veda can be called an exception to this characteristic; for Moses, Jesus, Muhammad, Confucius, and Gotama are all acknowledged by their followers as—at the very least—founders, sages, and prophets, both "prophet" and "sage" being unavoidable English translations of highly charged technical terms in the several originals. Because a sacred book purports to contain what the Holy said when It spoke to that person and what It did through that person, and hence what It is still speaking and still doing among us now, the identity of the founder or sage, howsoever that identity may be understood, is a key to the Sacred Book itself, as the founder comes out to address us from the sacred page.

The reader will usually recognize even without any prompting that in a religion that has a founder and in a sacred book believed to have come directly or indirectly from that founder, it is in the first instance the sayings of the founder-sage that occupy a special place. Some forms of sayings are nearly universal, while others are distinctive to a particular founder and a particular sacred book, and the reader should watch for both kinds. For example, as has been pointed out earlier, the title Analects, which means "miscellaneous selections," is now so specifically associated with the sayings of Confucius, although the word itself is of Greek origin, that we rarely use it in any other context. Yet "analects" would probably be applicable to at least some portions of each of the six volumes in this set. In the mouth of the founder-sage, even a miscellaneous collection of sayings takes on new force and special authority, sometimes because the founder is explicitly setting his sayings into opposition with current interpretations of the tradition and is claiming to have restored the original and authentic intention of the proverb or to have been granted new prophetic insight denied to his predecessors. The universality of the proverbial saying means that the parallels between the sayings of one founder and those of another, some of which are obvious and some of which are not as obvious as they might seem to the superficial observer, make the problems of translation referred to earlier especially acute in rendering such sayings across the boundaries of any two languages. For the key terms that are available to the translator have come out of the linguistic tradition, which is at the same time a religious tradition, of the translator and the readers. Should the translator strive for distinctiveness or for similarity? Part of the answer to that question lies in the attitude of each tradition toward the matter of distinctiveness itself. A religious commitment to the absolute and total uniqueness of the founder seems to lead to the necessary implication that any borrowings or even parallels are more apparent than real, or at any rate that they have taken place in only one direction. Yet if the founder-sage truly is the mouthpiece of the Holy, should there be anything shocking about the discovery that the founder's insights into the mystery of the Holy and into the meaning of human life reflect, and are reflected in, what other founders at other times and other places have also taught?

Part of the answer to these questions and thus also to the reader's interpretation of the founder's sayings lies in the life and deeds of the founder as the context for his sayings. To the faithful of any tradition, the founder stands not only as the master to be heard and obeyed, but as the model to be followed and imitated. To make sense of the life story of the founder-sage, the reader of a sacred book should learn to recognize the lessons that the authors or compilers of the Sacred Book seek to convey through their accounts of the founder's deeds. Thus the imperative of the Qur'ān "Do not oppress the orphan, and do not drive the beggar away" (93:9–10), an imperative that each of the other Sacred Books in this set echoes in its own way, has its counterpart in the Prophet's own acts of mercy; ultimately, as the superscriptions of the surahs read, it has its origins "in the name of Allah, most benevolent, ever-merciful." Because a persistent theme in the sayings of most founder-sages is the denunciation of hypocrisy—a phenomenon that somehow also seems to possess a universality of its own, cutting across all religious traditions and across the centuries—this correlation between word and deed is an important clue to the reading of the Sacred Book. "Do as I say *and* do as I do!" is what the founder-sage is saying to followers and readers.

Special importance, and for readers in a scientific age special difficulty, attaches to those deeds of various founder-sages that belong to the class of "miracles." For our purposes here it is, fortunately, not necessary to linger over the modern debates about how to define this problematical concept, except perhaps to stipulate that it does pertain to an action that surpasses or transcends or even contradicts the normal course of nature and in so doing conveys a meaning that at the same time surpasses or transcends or even contradicts the normal course of human knowledge. Such actions in the life of the founder-sage range very widely within and between the Sacred Books, from the early evidence of mental and physical prowess that marks a child prodigy to the manipulation of cosmic forces. Despite the evident interest of many believers in miracles for their own sake as an object of devotion or curiosity or superstition, the readers of any Sacred Book, be they believers or not, are well advised to avoid skipping over them or dismissing them as stunts or even tricks, for they are always more than that: for example, the Greek word "sēmeion," translated "miracle," means "sign-event." Upon encountering such stories about the wondrous deeds of the founder, a sophisticated reader will not ask, or at any rate will not ask only, whether or not this ever really happened. Rather, the question that ought to be uppermost in the mind of the reader should be: what significance attaches to the miracle story as part of the portrait of the founder-sage, and therefore how is it related both to the person of the founder and to the validation of the founder's message for his disciples and for other readers?

Discipleship is, then, another universal aspect of the religious phenomenon of the founder-sage. Even those highly skeptical modern readers who take a conspiratorial view of how religions have been founded and of how Sacred Books have been written find that they have to reckon with the fact of discipleship, if only to try, as Thomas Jefferson did in editing the New Testament, to rescue the founder from his disciples by separating the authentic words of the master from the inauthentic attributions invented by his followers. Sometimes these disciples are anonymous, and sometimes they have acquired an identity of their own. In the Analects of Confucius and in some of the other Sacred Books, as well as in other literature such as the Socratic dialogues of Plato, the disciple functions as a "straight man" whose questions and responses set up the master to deliver the message and to point the lesson; the disciple can also be a model and a norm of what the appropriate response to the words and deeds of the master ought to be. Yet a disciple is more than a mere reporter, more even than a pupil. For the disciple is one who has heard and accepted the summons of the sage and who has striven toward a life in accordance with that summons, thus establishing a pattern for future disciples. The full scope of discipleship depends partly on how the religion and its Sacred Book define the person of the founder-sage. Readers of the New Testament will recognize the particular significance of this key for the understanding of Christianity, in which the figure of the founder is normatively identified in the creed as "God from God, Light from Light, true God from true God," the Second Person of the Holy Trinity. No such metaphysical claims are made for Moses or Muhammad in the strict monotheisms of which they may be called "founders." The modern efforts to find parallels between Jesus Christ and either Confucius or Gotama Buddha, while endlessly fascinating because these figures have also eventually been endowed with a transcendent status, have generally ended in frustration or superficiality or both. In his own distinctive way, however, every one of these founders does lay a summons upon his disciples, and the Sacred Book comes to us from within the charmed circle of those who have accepted that summons.

From this we are to infer that we are confronting in any Sacred Book a special kind of history-telling as it goes on inside that charmed circle, one that is somehow different from ordinary history (whatever *that* may be). As Arthur Waley, our translator of the Confucian Analects, has observed, "Western scholars think it extremely important to discover exactly when people were born and exactly when they died," but such information tends to be of secondary importance for most of the Sacred Books in this set. Even when they do seem to be supplying chronological information that is intended to be precise, closer examination in the effort to correlate such information with "secular" history often yields results that turn out to be quite frustrating to the modern Western reader; we still cannot be sure just who the Pharaoh of the Exodus was. The source of the frustration lies in a worldview and a literary genre that historians and philosophers of religion generally characterize as "mythological." Contrary to the way this highly loaded term is often used, it does not imply, at least in the first instance, that the history about the founder-sage in the narrative of the Sacred Book did not really happen; for it definitely represents itself to us as "true," perhaps even more "true" than any of the two-dimensional history we read in textbooks and newspapers. But those quotation marks around the word "true" suggest the presence of a third or fourth dimension, without which we will get a distorted view of the sacred story.

No Sacred Book pretends to contain all the deeds and sayings of the founder. As we read a sacred book, therefore, we need to keep asking just why it was that this particular saying or deed was remembered as it was and what its connection may be with those that precede and follow it in the account. For if the account is not strictly chronological, it may nevertheless be logical in some more profound way. The logic of the compilation of sayings need not be that of the Aristotelian syllogism, proceeding from major premise to minor premise to conclusion, but may sometimes move in a lateral or a spiral direction. Thus the saying of Confucius the founder-sage with which the Analects open, "To learn and at due times to repeat what one has learnt, is that not after all a pleasure?" (1:1) becomes a kind of leitmotiv, which subsequent sayings substantiate even when they do not quote it. As the history of later interpretations, whether by believers or by scholars, amply documents, the contrasts or even contradictions between what the founder-sage says at one place and what he says at another provoke confusion, sometimes indeed offense, but they also provide the opportunity for critical reflection and for ingenious explanation (as, for example, our translator's note to the Qur'ān 4:3 illustrates). Living in an age when the practice of memorizing and reciting the classics is out of fashion in the schools, we may need to be reminded as we read the Sacred Books being presented here that large portions of each of them have been learned by heart and recited from memory. They were oral before they were written, and they went on being oral, perhaps even primarily oral, after they had been written; therefore they are meant to be heard, not merely to be read. That applies above all to the sayings of the founder, which often became the basic textbook material for primary education. In this way they also shape and inform much of the literature that has followed.

11

LITERATURE SACRED AND SECULAR

"Bible" simply means book (or books), "scripture" means writing, and "Qur'ān" means recitation. Every one of these words is used, sometimes even within the covers of the Sacred Books, for other books, writings, and recitations beyond the Book itself. Each of the six Sacred Books in this set, moreover, stands in a series not only with other Sacred Books, as it does here, but with the other books that belong to its own literary and linguistic tradition. Even readers who are firm believers, and especially readers who are not, have much to gain from approaching Sacred Books only as literature. Actually, it is naive to say "only as literature," for even so-called secular literature refuses to be seen that way. Is it really possible for anyone to read *King Lear* or *Oedipus Rex* or *Anna Karenina* "only as literature"? Indeed, the author of the last of those titles had some harsh things to say in his later years about writers, including himself when he wrote *Anna Karenina*, who do not pay sufficient attention to the religious and moral calling of fiction. Because religious faith claims to be a way of understanding and coping with the ultimate issues of life and death, other ways of doing this will inevitably overlap with it or conflict with it, and among such ways, the various arts—especially music, painting, and literature—have a long association with the sacred. Because literature so often deals with the sacred and because these six Sacred Books are all literature, the literary study of each of them occupies an important and legitimate place not alone in technical scholarship but in the approach of the general reader.

Not only has the translation of a sacred book often been the first monument of a written language, it has often gone on to become a classic and a model. For more than a thousand years throughout Western Europe, Jerome's translation of the Bible, the Vulgate, provided the imagery and vocabulary for lyric and epic, together with the linguistic and literary medium through which historiography, natural science, and sacred rhetoric enriched and shaped the literatures of various lands. For almost twice that long, the entire history of Sanskrit literature was similarly inspired and preoccupied with both the language and the themes of the Vedas, making any distinction between "secular literature" and "sacred literature" practically meaningless there. In the histories of world literature, therefore, a prominent place belongs to these and other Sacred Books, without which neither a native nor an outsider bent on becoming acquainted with the literary tradition can decipher it. The telling and retelling of materials from a sacred book is itself, in each of the groups shaped by these six collections of sacred scripture, a substantial chapter in the history of literature. Above all, the commentaries and paraphrases, such as the commentary on the Dhammapada that appears in our edition of it, constitute a literary form in their own right. But other forms of retelling loom large also as literary works. For readers of English, the best known of these is probably John Milton's *Paradise Lost*, in which the first three chapters of Genesis from the Tanakh provide a framework for poetic imagination, religious faith, and psychological speculation to present the human condition in a form that can speak also to those for whom the source of the original story does not have the status of normative Scripture.

Even more relevant to the readers of these *Sacred Writings* as a method is an examination of some of the principal literary genres appearing in the Sacred Books, for such an examination does provide guidance to reading and understanding them. It says something about Sacred Books as a genre, moreover, and it provides some justification for collecting them into a set of this kind, that with some degree of elasticity every one of these literary genres can be recognized in more than one of these Sacred Books, even though it may predominate in only one of them. As they stand, these literary forms often remain undifferentiated in the Sacred Books; but just as it is necessary in an ancient work of history such as *The History of the Peloponnesian War* by Thucydides to read the prose narratives differently from the way we read the speeches, so it is helpful to pay attention to the insights of the scholars into the poetry of Sacred Books, into prophetic utterance, into apocalyptic vision. The sheer amount of anguish that has been caused by controversy over Sacred Books might have been reduced significantly, for example, if it had been clearer to all sides just what the literary form of creation narratives is. The opening chapters of the Tanakh are not intended to provide a scientific explanation for the origin of things, but to affirm that God is the creator of the universe regardless of how it may have come into being.

Thus something very much like a collection of proverbs is present in the most widely separated cultures, frequently in the form of the traditions of the elders that have been passed down from generation to generation. Scholars have sometimes been able to chart the wanderings of various proverbs from one collection to another, across many religions, languages, and cultures; readers of these Sacred Books may have the same experience. Other sayings acquire distinctive forms, as in the "oracles" of Muhammad or the "parables" of Jesus or the "concrete illustrations" of Confucius. Although a proverb or apothegm will often depend for some of its effectiveness upon turns of language or plays on words virtually impossible to reproduce in a translation—how would one translate into any of the six languages represented here Benjamin Franklin's saying at the signing of the Declaration of Independence, "We must all hang together, or assuredly we shall all hang separately"?—it depends primarily upon its conformity with the widespread and even universal experiences or aspirations of humanity. Despite great diversity precisely on this score, Sacred Books may, and usually do, present themselves as the disclosure of something their hearers and readers did not know before, and thus at least in this respect as an insight into truth or sometimes even as a divine revelation. But even the highest claims to the credentials of revelation and inspiration—represented here probably by the Qur'ān, of which it is said, "We have sent down to you the Book containing the truth" (4:105)—do not prevent a sacred book from making an appeal to universal experiences and aspirations. Western readers of the Confucian Analects have frequently been struck by the appearance there of a proverbial saying, "Never do to others what you would not like them to do to you" (15:23), that closely resembles the Golden Rule attributed to Jesus Christ, "Always treat others as you would like them to treat you" (Matt. 7:12).

A second literary question in the reading of a Sacred Book is how to deal with its laws and rules of conduct. The question of legislation as a social and political force has been discussed in an earlier consideration of the relation between the Sacred Book and its people, but here it is the law as literature that concerns us. Study of the law as literature suggests that although the word "legislator" carries for us today the connotations of a deliberative process of compromise and give-and-take, those connotations are largely absent from the Sacred Books. Indeed, "lawgiver" would be a better title than "legislator" for the person of serene authority who issues these commandments. Related to that authority are the sanctions and promises the lawgiver attaches to his rules. Sometimes in each of the six Sacred Books these are the eminently this-worldly blessings of health and progeny, prosperity and peace, or the corresponding punishment of their lack. With degrees of specificity and intensity that vary greatly from one religion to another, however, each lawgiver also formulates his demands in a way that gives them some kind of transcendent and other-worldly dimension. Whatever the theological implications of this relation between the this-worldly and the other-worldly dimensions may be, it does affect the literary form of the law codes. As Robert Polzin, author of the chapter about the Book of Deuteronomy in *The Literary Guide to the Bible*, has observed, "The effect of the law code's composition, therefore, is to show us that the authoritative status of the Mosaic voice is *almost* indistinguishable from that of the voice of God" (italics his).

Yet another literary form that many Sacred Books either contain or presuppose is history and biography; within their respective national literatures they often are the earliest such narratives to have been recorded. As has been mentioned earlier, this is true preeminently of Sacred Books that trace the origin of their religion to a founder-sage. Therefore any account of a founder-sage will seem to partake of the nature of a biography. By modern standards, of course, such a "biography" will inevitably be disappointing, for some of the most fundamental information that any reader wants will be missing from it: we can, if we care to, learn more about the life story of any professional athlete or rock star of our own time than we can know about any one of the founders represented in these *Sacred Writings*. In studying the hallowed accounts of the Sacred Books, therefore, sensitive readers will constantly ask themselves what they are looking for in the historical narrative. On the other hand, the efforts of archaeologists to correlate their findings with the reports of the Sacred Books have frequently, though not invariably, illumined the history and literature that had been, before the digging, the only surviving relics of that ancient past. In the People's Republic of China, for example, archaeology and anthropology sometimes have, without any explicit desire to do anything of the kind, brought dramatic vindication of archaic tradition.

There is special significance to the genre of literature known as philosophy. The word "philosophy" has come to us from Greek, and so has our usual definition of the discipline itself. For the traditions represented by the first three of the Sacred Books in this set—the Tanakh, the New Testament, and the Qur'ān—the interaction between "philosophy" and "theology" has been a major element in the history of ideas. But for the three traditions in the second half of the set—the Analects, the Rig Veda, and the Dhammapada—such a dichotomy between "philosophy" and "theology" is at best artificial and at worst misleading. For despite the efforts mentioned earlier to find parallels to Jesus Christ in either Confucius or Gotama Buddha, the Western figure of whom those sages remind us the most frequently is in fact Socrates. The central character and theme in Fung Yu-Lan's *Short History of Chinese Philosophy*, therefore, is the sage Confucius; a standard work like that of A. B. Keith can carry the title *The Religion and Philosophy of the Veda and Upanishads*; and two widely read twentieth-century books, A. J. Bahm's *Philosophy of the Buddha* and T. R. V. Murti's *The Central Philosophy of Buddhism*, speak in the same accents about Gotama Buddha. That should perhaps suggest to secularized Westerners that religious faith and myth have been a more prominent factor also in the history of European philosophy than our textbooks sometimes tell us, as recent studies of Plato or Hegel have shown. Above all, it should be on the mind of anyone who reads the Sacred Books as literature.

Literature is only one of the arts, though obviously the most directly relevant to the study of Sacred Books as books. Ideally, a collection of *Sacred Writings* would be, in the modern vernacular, a "multimedia presentation," in which—keeping to the present order of the books— an elaborately wrought Haggadah, icons of the Virgin Mary, symbolic decorations of the Blue Mosque, Chinese silk paintings, sculptures of Vishnu, and statues of the Buddha from Southeast Asia, or the musical counterparts to each of these six, would all provide their own commentary on the sacred text. Even without such art works, however, the translations that appear here do at least attempt to capture some of the literary quality of the originals, in some passages more successfully than in others, and thus to inform, but also to inspire, those many readers who may find in aesthetic experience their nearest access to the Holy.

12

SPIRITUALITY AS PRAYER AND ACTION

Despite all the varieties of literary form it may encompass, every Sacred Book is a prayer book, or at any rate contains a prayer book. "Well awake they arise, at all times, the disciples of Gotama," says the Dhammapada (301), "in whom, both day and night, the mind delights in meditation." The theme of meditation by day and by night appears in more than one of these Sacred Books, for example in the Book of Psalms (1:2). Even readers who take them in hand out of idle curiosity must remind themselves that to the devout in each of these traditions the Sacred Book is intended, as the Rig Veda says, to "stimulate our prayers" (3:62.10). Thus it represents, at least in some respects, a conversation between the Holy and the believers, both individually and collectively. Yet it represents as well a summons from the Holy to a life of obedience, submission, and service.

Stated that way, this quality of the Sacred Book involves a distinction that is in its technical formulation a product of Greek thought, systematized by Aristotle, but one that can be applied with striking accuracy to a great variety of religious and philosophical traditions:

the distinction between the active life and the contemplative life. Although the monastic movements that have arisen at one time or another in each of these six religions have had to make a special point of drawing the line between the two, chiefly for the sake of protecting contemplation from the intrusive demands of the outside world, the very use in many languages of the words "the service of God" to denote both worship and action is evidence for the universality of the idea and for the universality of the problem. Even so antireligious a thinker as Karl Marx seems to be invoking it when he says, in his *Theses on Feuerbach* of 1845, "The philosophers have only *interpreted* the world, in various ways. Nevertheless, the point is to *change* it." Interestingly, Marx, connoisseur of revolution though he was, spent much of his own life studying and "interpreting" the world, leaving it to other revolutionaries to do the actual "changing." Two members of the body, the eye and the hand, that have distinct tasks but must work together for the body to function properly; two points of the religious compass, the one at a fixed position and the other drawing circles everywhere; the intake and the output of the metabolism of faith; the *cantus firmus* in the lower clef and cadenzas in the upper clef—in some of these metaphors and in other similar ones, the subsequent interpreters of these six Sacred Books have related the active life to the contemplative life by distinguishing them, sometimes even distinguishing them sharply, yet without totally separating them.

Any prayer book, and especially a sacred book used as a prayer book, will manifest one characteristic of prayer pointed out by Friedrich Heiler, a sensitive and learned modern student of the phenomenon of prayer in many religious traditions: in what they pray and in how they pray, the world religions are at one and the same time the closest together, closer than in doctrine or in morality or in other ritual, but also the farthest apart. The readers of these Sacred Books would do well to keep that characteristic of prayer in mind. Above all, they must not forget that the Book does primarily have the praying individual and the praying community in mind, and only secondarily (if at all) the inquiring reader, that it was written for worship more than for research. When the opportunity presents itself, during travel or in a travelogue, to witness a sacred book in actual use by a praying community in a feast or festival, such a picture truly is, as the cliché says, worth a thousand words, even a thousand of the words in the Sacred Book. In such a setting it becomes clear that the "paradox of understanding" mentioned earlier manifests itself with special force in worship and prayer. When, as the Dhammapada says (301), the disciples of Gotama, well awake, arise at all times and delight in meditation, both day and night, the experience of watching saffron-robed Buddhist monks at their prayers can seem very strange to a Western observer. Yet someone would have to be hopelessly bigoted as well as religiously tone-deaf not to be able to find somewhere in each of these six Sacred Books the accents of a spirituality to which it is possible for human beings of various backgrounds to respond and in which it is possible for them to pray, as deep calleth unto deep, across all the boundaries of all the world religions.

Part of the strangeness of the worship life of other religious traditions involves their specific practices and techniques of meditation, for example, the prayer wheel or rosary beads—the modern English word "bead" comes from the Old English word for "prayer"—accompanied by the recitation of verses from a sacred text. Nor are the gestures and postures of prayer the same everywhere, although some customs, such as kneeling for prayer and facing eastward to the rising sun, have appeared in many otherwise unrelated traditions. It is also a well-nigh universal tendency of religious groups to attach great importance to the precise details of worship practice, including the absolute accuracy of the very words being recited from the Sacred Book. In the absence of comprehensive and reliable statistics, it is probably fair to estimate that more controversies and schisms have arisen over these details than over any theological doctrine in the book. As uninitiated readers reflect on a sacred book, therefore, it is important to remember that a phrase or sentence over which they can pass lightly may have been the object of intense passions or hatreds in the past or may still be, and even more important to keep in mind that, as the faithful have meditated and prayed over the hallowed text, they have sometimes been transported in religious ecstasy to the very vision of the Holy.

Probably the most universal of all devotional practices in the use of the Sacred Book is song. Not only is much of the sacred text a poem, as we have had occasion to point out several times, but it is a poem that has been set to music. For many passages, the song came before the written text and was transmitted from one generation of believers to the next in the form of a chant or hymn. As is evident from the very title *Hymns of the Rig Veda*, used not only in our set but in other translations, that applies especially to this Sacred Book of Hinduism. "Our songs and holy hymns go forth to Agni," the faithful sing there, "seeking the God and asking him for riches" (7:10.3). And again, a few hymns later, "Bring song and hymn to Agni. . . . Like an oblation on the grass, to please him, I bring this to Vaiśvānara, hymn-inspirer" (7:13.1). Therefore when the Hebrew psalmist exhorts, "Sing to the Lord a new song, sing to the Lord, all the earth" (Ps. 96:1), the new song is in fact a very old song, but one that becomes new each time a new voice sings it for the first time or each time a genius like Johann Sebastian Bach sets it to music. Even modern technology, unfortunately, has no easy way of allowing the reader of a text to hear its melodies while looking at its words, although for at least some of the words in some of these Sacred Books that is far easier than it used to be. Absent such technological props, those who read one of these Sacred Books only as a written text—like those who read such epics as the *Iliad* and the *Odyssey*—will read it with greater understanding if throughout their reading they are aware of a tune that is continually being sung *sotto voce* beneath the hearing and seeing of the words themselves.

Even the most extreme contemplatives, however, remain conscious of their obligations to others as part of their obligation to God. The very act of writing down a sacred book in response to a divine command or inspiration, and then of copying it over and over again for later readers, implies that the sharing of the vision is an essential component of the spirituality derived from the vision. In the words of one of the greatest of Western contemplative thinkers, Thomas Aquinas, "As it is better to enlighten than merely to shine, so it is better to give to others the fruits of one's contemplation than merely to contemplate." That accent reflects the emphasis also of the Sacred Books. Thus Confucius warns in the Analects (4:25): "Moral force never dwells in solitude; it will always bring neighbors." The Gospel denounces as a "worthless, lazy servant" one who, upon being "given one bag of gold went off and dug a hole in the ground, and hid his master's money" instead of putting it to use (Matt. 25:14–30). Similarly, the Qur'ān promises "a higher place on the Day of Reckoning" specifically to "those who keep from evil and follow the straight path" (2:212). And Moses did not remain on Mount Sinai contemplating the ineffable mystery of the Holy, but came down from the mountain bearing the tables of the Law in which the will of the Holy for human life was set forth (Ex. 19:25). Indeed, so pervasive is the moral imperative throughout the world religions that philosophers of religion have repeatedly sought, especially since the Enlightenment of the eighteenth century, to reduce the content of religion to its ethical requirements and, in doing so, to show that in their essentials all the religions are finally alike, with only the trivia of ritual or dogma separating them. While such a reductionism has repeatedly proved to be misguided and simpleminded, it does express the valid and universal insight of all the Sacred Books and of all the world religions, that, as the New Testament expresses it, "faith divorced from action is dead" (James 2:26).

Theocentric and other-worldly though the religious definition of spirituality sometimes tends to be, that does not in any way negate the emphasis on this world and its responsibilities. The Tanakh reminds its readers: "God is in heaven and you are on earth" (Eccles. 5:1). Yet of the six Sacred Books presented here, it is probably above all the Confucian Analects in which that emphasis is articulated. Thus when someone asked about the meaning of ritual, "the Master said, 'I do not know'" (3:11), and the phrase "I do not know" sounds over and over when metaphysical issues are raised (5:7). But the Master can also explicitly enumerate "four of the virtues" found in a model of the good life: "In his private conduct he was courteous, in serving his master he was punctilious, in providing for the needs of the people he gave them even more than their due, in exacting service from the people he was just" (5:15). A modern reader who puts two or more of these Sacred Books side by side will repeatedly find large areas of similarity, especially in such prescriptions as these for the life of virtue and justice. The ground of hopes for world peace and for harmony within one neighborhood or nation lies in such similarity, and in the willingness of those who differ fundamentally on ultimate metaphysical and theological issues nevertheless to achieve a kind of ethical ecumenism in their common acceptance of these norms. Almost anyone who lives in the twentieth century anywhere in the world would be pleased to have as a neighbor or as a public official someone who lived up to the deepest meaning of the basic moral tenets that are set out in any of these six Sacred Books. As one quasi-proverbial version of a formula for civic and religious peace has it, "In essentials unity, in nonessentials liberty, and in all things charity."

As one reads a sacred book, it is nevertheless not only the individual as neighbor or public official but an entire community that is often being addressed. That is why this introduction has suggested that it is appropriate to apply the term "people of the Book" not only to Judaism, for which the Qur'ān originally used it, but to the Christianity and Islam that share some of that Book, as well as to

Confucianism, Hinduism, and Buddhism, for each of which, albeit in different ways, there is a corporate as well as an individual message in the moral tenets conveyed by the Sacred Book. The many and varied cultures that have been shaped by these six Sacred Books bear evidence to how a sacred book can define the entire character of a people—its work habits, its definition of beauty and goodness, its dietary customs, its sexual mores, its view of history—for those who no longer share its fundamental beliefs as well as for those who adhere to its traditions. Each of the six, therefore, has also faced in the modern world the question of what is called in shorthand "theocracy," namely, whether those who do not believe may be compelled to submit to rules of life that come from the Sacred Book (in the order in which they appear here): kosher laws in the state of Israel, Sunday "blue laws" in the United States, the "Qur'ānic privilege" of polygamy in Egypt, the sacredness of the family in China, the reverence for cattle in India, the special status of monks in Southeast Asia. Some of the most divisive issues in many modern societies come from debates over this problem of theocracy. Howsoever those issues may be addressed, a minimum prerequisite for dealing with them would seem to be that all citizens, believers and unbelievers and semibelievers, gain an understanding of the context out of which the issues arise. And so, yet again: "Understandest thou what thou readest?" and "How can I without someone to guide me?"

FOR FURTHER READING
AND REFERENCE

Achtemeier, Paul J. ed. *Harper's Bible Dictionary*. San Francisco: Harper and Row, 1985.

Ackroyd, P. R. et al, eds. *The Cambridge History of the Bible*. 3 vols. Cambridge: Cambridge University Press, 1963–70.

Alter, Robert, and Frank Kermode, eds. *The Literary Guide to the Bible*. Cambridge, MA: Harvard University Press, 1987.

Bahm, A. J. *Philosophy of the Buddha*. New York: Harper and Brothers, 1958.

Ballou, Robert O., ed. *The Bible of the World*. New York: The Viking Press, 1939.

Carter, John Ross. *Dhamma: Western Academic and Sinhalese Buddhist Interpretations*. Tokyo: Hokuseido Press, 1978.

Eliade, Mircea. *The Sacred and the Profane*. Translated by Willard R. Trask. New York: Harcourt, Brace and Company, 1959.

Fung Yu-Lan. *A Short History of Chinese Philosophy*. New York: Free Press, 1976.

Heiler, Friedrich. *Prayer: A Study in the History and Psychology of Religion*. Translated by S. McComb and J. E. Park. New York: Oxford University Press, 1932.

Hodgson, Marshall G. G. *The Classical Age of Islam*. Volume 1 of *The Venture of Islam*. Chicago: The University of Chicago Press, 1974.

Jurji, Edward J., ed. *The Great Religions of the Modern World*. Princeton: Princeton University Press, 1946.

Keith, A. B. *The Religion and Philosophy of the Veda and Upanishads*. Cambridge, MA: Harvard University Press, 1925.

Kitagawa, Joseph M. *Religions of the East*. Philadelphia: Westminster Press, 1960.

Lau, D.C., ed. and tr. Confucius. *The Analects*. Harmondsworth: Penguin Books, 1979.

Murti, T. R. V. *The Central Philosophy of Buddhism*. London: George Allen and Unwin, 1955.

Nasr, Seyyed Hossein. *Ideals and Realities of Islam*. London: Unwin Hyman Ltd., 1967.

O'Flaherty, Wendy Doniger, ed. and tr. *The Rig Veda: An Anthology*. Harmondsworth: Penguin Books, 1981.

Ogden, Schubert M. *Is There Only One True Religion or Are There Many?* Dallas, TX: Southern Methodist University Press, 1992.

Pelikan, Jaroslav. *The Christian Tradition: A History of the Development of Doctrine*. 5 vols. Chicago: The University of Chicago Press, 1971–1989.

————, ed. *The World Treasury of Modern Religious Thought*. Boston: Little, Brown and Company, 1990.

Radhakrishnan, Sarvepalli. *Eastern Religions and Western Thought*. 2d ed. London and New York: Oxford University Press, 1940.

————, and Charles A. Moore, eds. *A Source Book in Indian Philosophy*. Princeton: Princeton University Press, 1957.

Rahman, Fazlur. *Islam*. 2d ed. Chicago: The University of Chicago Press, 1979.

Schwartz, Benjamin I. "Confucius: The Vision of the *Analects*." In *The World of Thought in Ancient China*, 56–134. Cambridge, MA: Harvard University Press, 1985.

Smith, Huston. *The Religions of Man*. New York: Harper and Brothers, 1958.

Smith, Wilfred Cantwell. *Towards a World Theology: Faith and the Comparative History of Religion*. Philadelphia: Westminster Press, 1981.

Suzuki, Daisetz Teitarū. *Essays in Zen Buddhism*. Tokyo: The Matsugaoka Bunko, 1971.

Wright, Arthur F. *Studies in Chinese Buddhism*. New Haven: Yale University Press, 1990.

Enjoy Your Garden

FLOWERING TREES AND SHRUBS

IN COLOUR

Edited by
F B Stark, C B Link and E L Packer

ORBIS PUBLISHING · LONDON

Contents

Picture Credits: C. Mariorossi: cover; Archivio I.G.D.A.: 3, 4, 20, 28, 29, 32, 33, 34, 39, 41, 45, 46, 52, 54, 57, 58, 62, 88, 112, 113; M. Bavestrelli: 17, 31, 69, 111, 139; C. Bevilacqua: 24, 51, 53, 63, 81, 115, 116, 118, 122, 123, 127, 135, 154, 162, 166; Bravo: 73; E.P.S.: 1, 23, 25, 38, 48, 74, 82, 83, 84, 85, 91, 92, 93, 97, 98, 103, 106, 109, 110, 126, 143, 144, 146, 147, 149, 150, 155, 158, 172; R. Longo: 77, 99, 105, 121, 125, 140, 141; A. Margiocco: 37; P. Martini: 124, 161; G. P. Mondino: 5, 16, 19, 21, 22, 27, 30, 35, 40, 42, 43, 44, 47, 49, 50, 55, 56, 60, 65, 68, 70, 71, 72, 75, 79, 87, 89, 94, 101, 107, 108, 114, 117, 119, 142, 148, 153, 159, 160, 163, 164, 165, 168, 169, 170, 173; P 2: 61, 78, 90, 128, 129, 130, 131, 132, 133, 134, 136, 137, 138, 145, 151, 152, 171; M. Pedone: 80, 96, 156, 157, 167; A. Sella: 9, 10, 11, 13, 15; G. Tomsich: 100, 104; S. Viola: 64, 66, 86, 102, 120.

Adapted from the Italian of Gian Paolo Mondino
Edited by Francis C. Stark, Conrad B. Link and Edwin Packer

© Orbis Publishing Limited, London 1974
© Istituto Geografico De Agostini, Novara 1969
Printed in Italy by IGDA, Novara

SBN 85613 166 0

Trees and shrubs
in the history of gardens

Trees have always held a fascination for man. Why this should be is a matter for conjecture. They impress with their strength and they display an infinite variety of shapes, forms and habits of growth. They provide a link with the past. And there are other reasons why man values the presence of trees. For many thousands of years they have provided him with timber for housing, furniture and fencing, for ships and implements, and for the manufacture of all kinds of useful and ornamental objects.

Throughout history they have played a part in man's religious life as the sacred groves of the Greeks, the Romans, the Gauls, and the Germans attest. In Britain forests of huge oaks were revered and protected by the Druids before the Roman invasion. Unfortunately most of the ancient oaks in Britain have disappeared but there are still protected groves of venerable yews and beeches. The Greeks consecrated the oak to their god Jupiter; the tree was also sacred to the Celtic people, as well as to the Germans who dedicated it to Thor. That these beliefs persisted as superstitions even with the advent of Christianity is shown by a decree of Charlemagne of 789 A.D. (which remained unobserved) ordering the cutting of the sacred woods, and by the numerous decrees, promulgated by Councils in Germany and Britain until the thirteenth century, against those who practised divination beneath the trees. The fact that modern man also finds something esoteric and noble in trees is demonstrated by our planting of trees in parks or forests as living memorials to those killed in war.

In the brief historical introduction that follows, the development of landscape architecture is described, and the role played in various epochs by trees and shrubs—which are the basic, coordinating elements of gardens—will be noted.

From antiquity we have evidence of Egyptian gardens with a regular design, of the Hanging Gardens of Babylon with straight paths, of the more natural Greek gardens with tree groves and flower beds. We know more about Roman gardens based on their representation in mosaics, and by archaeological finds and writings. Their centre was usually a small piazza with fountains, crisscrossed by rectilinear paths like the streets of their cities.

Flanking the lanes of cypresses, pines, oaks, palms, olives and lindens were hedges of rosemary, myrtle and box with clumps of holly and laurel; here and there were such decorative elements as vases, statues, small temples, colonnades and fountains. Gardeners pruned shrubs into the most varied topiary forms, sometimes transforming them into works of art.

Many centuries before Christ the Chinese garden with its irregular design was well developed, and descriptions of it have come to us with examples handed down from imperial and monastic gardens. The elements of the garden were rather complex; a skilful use was made of water, and thought was given to the disposition of buildings, rocks, grottoes, hills and panoramas so that the vistas were diversified—all of which contributed to the enchantment of the view and stirred the imagination. The trees and shrubs most often used were the flowering cherries, dwarf maples, magnolias, camelias, bamboo and hydrangeas.

The Japanese garden is influenced by the Chinese; while simple in structure, it is often symbolic of man's emotions. Gardens of dwarf firs are typical of this form.

In the Moslem garden, of which eloquent testimony remains in the Alhambra at Granada, great importance was attached to water which was used not only for aesthetic purposes but also to moderate the temperature in the courtyards. The luxurious garden of the Generalife still exists.

During the Middle Ages, with the difficulties and insecurity of the times, gardens were maintained inside the walls of castles and monasteries and became functional with plantings of fruits and vegetables. A creation of the Renaissance is the Italian garden, wherein man bent nature to his ends, adapting the landscape to the new spirit of the times. These gardens are notable for a geometrical rigidity of design, a heritage of ancient Rome. The Florentine garden of the fifteenth century, situated on the plain, was characterized by the evergreen hedges defining formal beds and the use of shrubs, as well as trees with even tops, to form various designs. The hedges, the vines on the pergolas, the shrubs outlining the mazes and the trees with high trunks were pruned; trees formed groups with a constructive purpose. The garden was embellished with statues, vases,

4

sarcophagi (a relic of Roman gardens), fountains and seats. In the sixteenth century, Italian gardens took on a more ornamental character; an important innovation was their use to complement the home in the countryside.

In the Roman garden of the sixteenth century, constructed on a slope, these elements remained but they were set picturesquely on terraces, each level connected to the others by flights of stairs; here water acquired greater decorative importance in fountains, streams and waterfalls. In the seventeenth century the baroque elements were accentuated and greater importance was given to construction, using fountains, nymphs, grottoes, and colonnades.

The rigid scheme of the Italian garden was taken and made more elaborate in the French garden, designed on rolling terrain, particularly through the work of Le Notre (1613–1700) in which the important element of perspective was introduced. Here trees and groves were kept distant from buildings to give a broad sweep to the panorama, while in the foreground were placed flower beds, lawns, beds of shrubs and pools of water with statues and fountains.

The central walk, intersected by side paths, was laid out on the long axis, with groves interposed. The beds often contained plants that could be trimmed into geometrical forms; the same principle was applied in the case of the vines, hedges and mazes. The buildings in the garden took the form of informal or formal pavilions. The French garden spread to Germany, Austria and Italy during the eighteenth century; in the latter country it became popular in regions less influenced by the Italian school.

The English garden, pictorial or natural, was a romantic reaction to the cold academism of earlier styles; influenced by Chinese gardens, it sought to relate to the surrounding countryside. The guiding principle of this garden was no longer the imposition of artificiality but a blending with nature, suitably proportioned with finishing touches and embellishments. Symmetry, straight lines and pruning were thus abandoned. Great importance was given to well cared for carpets of grass and curving paths, and to water reproducing natural springs, brooks and lakes. Specimen trees were emphasized, and groves were of an irregular shape, each usually composed of a single species. In these gardens a great number of exotic plants, at that time only recently discovered, were introduced.

In the nineteenth century eclecticism triumphed in garden design as it did in architecture without, however, often attaining a valid artistic mix. In this period, orangeries and conservatories, already in existence in the eighteenth century, became widespread.

In the present century there has been an increase in the number of public gardens in cities and a decrease in private gardens. Gardens once were the privilege of a few; today they perform a social function in being accessible to all citizens and especially to children. They are important at a time like today when city life is becoming more and more

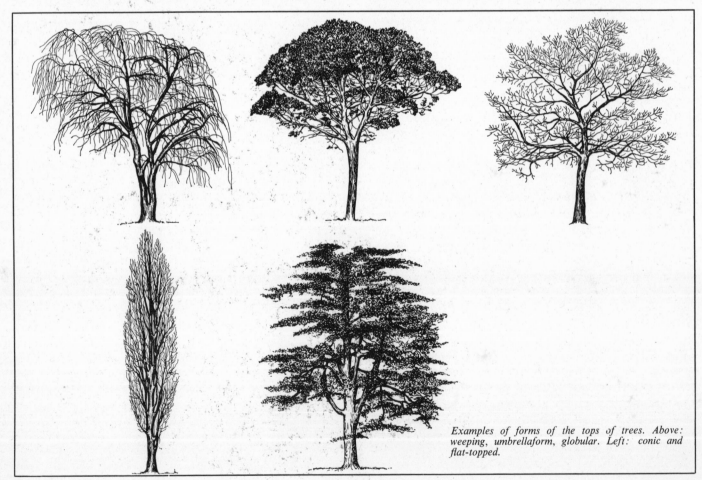

Examples of forms of the tops of trees. Above: weeping, umbrellaform, globular. Left: conic and flat-topped.

artificial. In addition to their aesthetic value, the function performed by trees and plants—that of ameliorating the polluted air of the urban conglomeration—is of importance to health. In recent decades we have witnessed a deterioration of the environment due to highway construction, industrialization and housing, and the balance should be redressed.

The use of trees and shrubs

Trees and shrubs form the backbone of the garden; thus their choice and setting are of the greatest importance. In general terms, these woody plants must be suited to the surroundings, not only to avoid damage from the weather, but also so as not to introduce plants that do not blend well with the landscape. The distinction between trees and shrubs is not always clear cut, because species of trees which are large under normal conditions become shrubs when growing near the altitudinal or latitudinal limits of the species. So the aspen can be found 100 feet tall at a low altitude but is no more than a 4 feet shrub-size in the high Rocky Mountains. The form, not the size, is the deciding feature.

To make the design stand out, trees and shrubs should, if possible, leave a vista of the surrounding countryside in order to give a background that, visually and aesthetically, seems to spread from the garden to the horizon, creating the illusion of greater breathing space. When a large park is planned, it is best to leave the entrance free and facing the view, with a broad carpet of grass directly in front and with those trees of great height in the distance. In level areas one can give the impression of a more rolling landscape by alternating tall groups of plants with shorter ones. On the other hand, if the ground already has considerable slope, this may be softened visually by the use of the shorter plants on the heights and the taller trees on the lower sites.

The choice of plants depends on their particular characteristics; a broadleaf gives shade in hot weather but is bare in winter, while conifers give little shade but keep their ornamental effect in winter. With deciduous types, however, the fine web of the branches and the particular effect of an interesting bark, no longer hidden by leaves, can become aesthetically appealing during winter. The relationship between trees and shrubs must be undertaken with care to avoid extreme contrasts of colour and form, or a complete lack of contrast. Thus plants of a particular form, towering or weeping, should be kept apart, while collections of shrubs (for example, dwarf firs, or those with coloured tops) may be grouped. It is also very important to choose species with an eye to their future development; thus, if a garden is of limited size, it should be designed for plants of restrained height to achieve a good aesthetic effect with time. Finally, it is necessary to restrict the choice to a certain number of species for planting and grouping, so that you do not overload the garden with so many kinds as to make it resemble a botanical garden.

Trees

Trees may be set out individually as specimens or in groups, to create groves and green arches, to form curtains and paths. In the first case we are dealing in general with a tree of great stature (although not always) which has aesthetic characteristics that attract the eye to its particular shape, the form or colour of the bark, the shape and colour of the leaves, the flowers, or the fruit, or its appearance in a particular season. The thickets or groups, composed of trees of lesser stature, can serve as protection to delicate plants or flower beds, to prepare the eye for changes of view, to give tones of colour, to give movement to areas that otherwise would be monotonous, and to act as screens.

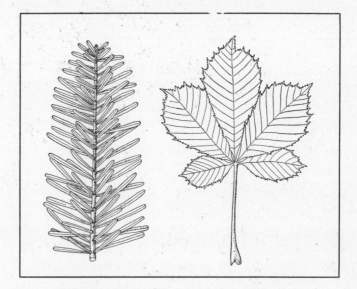

Examples of needle leaves (conifer) at left, and broadleaves.

To form groves, the preference will doubtless be given to plants native to the region or perhaps, to obtain an effect in shorter time, to some rapidly growing conifer. The green "vaults" or arches—decorative covered paths or roads that require considerable maintenance—are excellent for the entrances to large gardens. They must be created with trees that permit heavy pruning. If maximum height is desired, the choice may be made from among plane trees, elms, horse chestnuts and lindens; if a lower height is wanted, the hornbeam is preferred. Screening plants are, in practice, high hedges, and these are discussed later.

Paths and roads

Whether in the urban or the non-urban landscape, lanes of tall trees add an aesthetic note. There has recently been much discussion over the propriety of planting trees outside cities because of the disadvantages they create for high-speed automobile traffic on narrow winding roads. In cities, certainly, trees beautify, provide shade, and improve the air in that plants, by photosynthesis, take in carbon dioxide, the waste of human respiration and of combustion, and return oxygen to the air. In addition, the broadleaved trees regulate the temperature of a restricted atmosphere by the emission of water vapour and the absorption of heat.

History gives us examples of urban plantings as far back as Roman days, when the streets of the patricians were embellished with them. In the Middle Ages and later there is no mention of lanes until 1616, when at the insistence of Marie de Medici a lane of elms was planted at the Cours-la-Reine in Paris. In 1650, a lane of lindens and walnuts was planted in Berlin. In France, the planting of trees along city streets became general during the First Empire.

The distance of trees from the front of dwellings and from the edge of the street should be sufficient to ensure that drastic or too frequent pruning will not be required. The proper spacing of trees along the rows and their position, if they are set in parallel rows, is very important. For trees that grow to 75 feet, the spacing should be about 40 feet; for those 40 feet high, 27 feet; for those 20 feet high, 12 feet, and so on—interpolating for intermediate heights and increasing the distance in proportion if there is more than one row. In this instance the trees can be set out in squares, to form rows in two directions, or at the points of equilateral triangles, forming rows in three directions. If shade is desired quickly, trees may be placed at half distance, every other one being removed later to allow for natural growth.

The spacing of trees depends also on the form assumed by their tops and on their shape; towering trees with soaring branches, such as the Lombardy poplar, have a close-gathered head and so may be planted more closely than indicated above.

In the selection of species it is wise to keep in mind the climatic and soil requirements. If, as is usual, shade is wanted, one must plant broadleaved trees with a broad, dense top (plane trees, elms, maples, lindens, horse chestnut, etc.). If only a particular aesthetic effect is desired, one will plant conifers or such flowering trees and shrubs as red bud, mimosa, *Paulownia*, apple, plum, magnolia, crape-myrtle, or those with ornamental fruit (e.g. *Pyracantha*).

Trees that are heavily scented when in bloom can be troublesome to some persons as can the unpleasant odour coming from the leaves of the ailanthus and the fruit of the ginkgo.

Of the dangers besetting trees on city streets, some are almost specific to the kind of tree. Others are due to such extraneous factors as gas leaks, deposits of dust, or poisonous gases in the atmosphere. With underground gas leaks the roots become asphyxiated, and when this happens the soil must be thoroughly aerated before replanting. Dust and gas in the air physically obstruct the stomata at first, next "burning" the leaves. Some conifers are particularly susceptible to air pollutants. The tips of their needles turn reddish-brown and wither. Among broadleaved trees the chestnut, the linden and the elm are susceptible because of their rough or hairy leaves; those with smooth leaves or leaves that move easily in the breeze are less harmed.

Shrubs

The choice of shrubs ranges over a great number of plants of the most diverse requirements and ornamental qualities. There are three main categories: those for flowers, those for fruit and those for foliage. Bear in mind, however, that there are no strict lines between them.

The first group which stand out better in masses against a grassy background, provide us with a good selection that will keep the garden in flower the whole summer, with some actual winter bloom if the site has good exposure (such as *Chimonanthus fragrans, Hamamelis mollis, Erica carnea*). Beginning with the earliest kinds gradually coming into bloom in spring, we have forsythia and *Chaenomeles japonica*, then various viburnums, spirea and dogwood (the splendid *Cornus florida*), azaleas, rhododendrons, lilacs, *Deutzia*, mock orange and hawthorn.

These are followed by the summer flowering of *Buddleia, Ceanothus, Hibiscus*, some spireas and others. Among the shrubs that flower at the same time, one should give consideration to the location of diverse types, so their colours do not clash but create a harmonious setting (this is especially important for rhododendrons).

Fruit also gives a bright note to shrubs, especially if it persists over winter, as with *Pyracantha, Contoneaster* and some hollies.

Hedges

The functions of hedges in the garden are manifold, and these must be discussed at some length when dealing with suitable species. Hedges, especially of evergreens, had their greatest success in the Renaissance and the sixteenth and seventeenth centuries, as true architectural elements of the Italian garden and, later, of the French garden. Today, hedges (high screens or low plantings) are used to outline the limits of the property, to divide the garden into parts, to screen walls that disrupt the setting and to protect against wind.

Plants suitable for hedges are mostly of shrubby growth; they should have dense foliage and be able to tolerate pruning. Choice should be made with ecological criteria in mind; some of these plants tolerate shade well, others want more sun, and still others must be used only in sheltered positions not too cold in winter. Insofar as possible, evergreens are chosen so that the screen is maintained throughout the year. The choice of species is long and certainly is not exhausted by the examples that follow: the very hardy privet; the low but ornamental barberry, *Berberis Thunbergii*; the numerous *Cotoneasters*; the *Pyracanthas*, ornamental in fruit and foliage; *Chaenomeles japonica*; *Elaeagnus pungens*; laurel; spirea; hibiscus; box, rather elegant, but slow-growing; holly; and cherry laurel. For high hedges (screens) choose from taller species such as hornbeam, Arizona cypress, yew, arborvitae, and holm oak. Among plants suited only to the warmest maritime localities of southern England, or to the greenhouse, choose from *Pittosporum*, myrtle, rosemary, oleander, croton, arbutus, holm oaks, laurel, and viburnum—all evergreen. Hardy varieties of some of these can be obtained.

If an impassable hedge is desired, choose spiny plants such as hawthorn, *Citrus trifoliata*, and *Maclura pomifera* or, for warmer areas, Christ's thorn (*Paliurus spina-Christi*). After the planting of hedges, it is necessary to cut back the tops to encourage lateral branches and to thicken foliage, particularly at the base (this is done two or three times a year). When the hedge is finally shaped, it is sheared to keep it attractive, the frequency depending on the species and its growth rate.

Shrubs for the rock garden

Although the majority of plants grown in the rock garden are herbaceous or somewhat bushy, it is good to introduce some shrubs to make the total setting livelier. The rock garden seems ready-made for the limited space we have today for our gardens, and its lack of popularity may be that it is difficult to construct.

The rock garden is an arrangement of rocks (siliceous or calcareous according to the requirements of the plants one wants to grow), among the clefts of which are placed plants indigenous to rocky surroundings and primarily from the mountains.

The choice of woody plants for this purpose are those of limited development and slow growth. They must not give too much shade to herbaceous plants, nor should they make the environment unnatural; the limited size of most rock gardens rules out large-growing types, which, of course, would not find conditions suitable in the rock clefts, pockets of earth and small terraces.

Suitable shrubby plants may be found among the natural flora (Mugo pine, *Erica carnea*, the azaleas), and some conifers have wonderful shapes suited to this purpose, including *Chamaecyparis*, with its diverse species and numerous cultivars, cone-shaped, globular, or weeping in habit, and dense, compact top, often of varied colours. Among these are: *Chamaecyparis obtusa* var. *ericoides*, purple in winter; *C. obtusa* var. *nana*; *C. obtusa* var. *pygmaea*, bronze-green; and *C. obtusa* var. *tetragona*, with golden, mosslike foliage.

Another group of conifers suited to rock gardens is the junipers, of rather variable shape. *Picea Abies*, too, the common spruce used as Christmas trees, has various cultivars useful here, as do the arborvitae. The dwarf yew may be used for shaded slopes and northern exposures. Among the broadleaved evergreens are some rhododendrons; *Cistus* (only for sheltered positions); *Berberis buxifolia*, with orange flowers and dark blue berries; and the various *Cotoneasters*. Among deciduous broadleaves, *Cytisus* hybrids, various brooms, some daphnes and *Helianthemum*, some *Ceanothus*, *Hypericum calycinum*, and *Potentilla fruticosa* are recommended.

Propagation, planting, and culture

The propagation of plants is the basis of the nursery industry; the techniques are being refined with time, aided in recent years by artificial illumination, water mists in greenhouses, low-volume irrigation, mechanical transplanters, the use of growth regulators, insecticides, fungicides and herbicides.

Propagation is fundamentally of two types: sexual (by seed) and asexual (or vegetative) including division, layering, air layering, cuttings and grafting.

Propagation by seed

The specimens that result from the propagation of plants by seed are generally very vigorous, but the method is limited to the reproduction of species in which the desired characters do not vary and breed true, and are transmitted genetically. Some characters are reproduced only by vegetative means.

Male and female cells, known as gametes, in the cell are responsible for the reproductive process; the female developing to produce the new plant when given the impetus by the male.

After harvest, seeds are usually sown in sand or a soil mixture. Some species, however, must spend the winter in the ground to permit the seed to truly ripen; the same result may be obtained by refrigerating the seeds in a moist peat moss medium until growth begins, after which they should be planted in soil. Certain seeds with a hard shell must be scarified before planting. Other seeds, such as mimosa and *Acer palmatum*, are soaked in warm water before sowing to ensure rapid germination.

Regarding the soil medium for the seedlings, a loamy mixture is best to get good root development. The soil should be easy to till after rain, and must be well-drained to prevent root rot. Irrigation must be provided as well as a suitable system for eliminating excess water.

Seeds are sown in spring, when the soil warms suitably, usually in rows to simplify weeding; depth is in relation to the size of the seeds—in general a depth 5 times the diameter except for very large seeds. Very small seeds, such as those of rhododendrons, should not be covered with soil, or only lightly. If broadcast sowing must be done, choose days without wind and mix small seeds with sand or other material to make sowing more uniform. The seedlings must be given water and shade, and diseases, insects and weeds must be controlled. Weeding is done by hand, by mechanical implements (tillers, motorized cultivators), or by chemical means (herbicides or weed killers)—but is unnecessary if sowing is in sterilized soil. After some months it is necessary to transplant the seedlings to provide more space for the plants and to let the roots develop. Some care must be taken in digging the plants to ensure that the roots are not injured or allowed to get dry. At this time only the better seedlings are chosen.

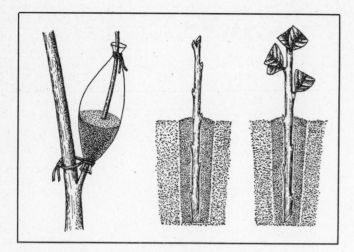

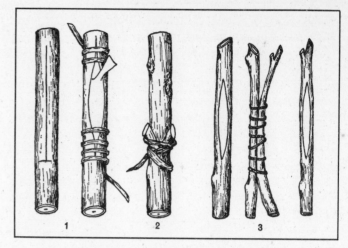

Vegetative reproduction; (from left), air layering, hardwood cutting, soft-wood cutting.

Grafting: (1) budding; (2) cleft graft; (3) approach graft.

Vegetative propagation

Division is a simple method but is not used in large-scale operations. It is limited to shrubs that produce rooted side shoots. Examples of this are *Kerria japonica, Hypericum calycinum, Rhus typhina, Chaenomeles japonica, Deutzia, Philadelphus,* bamboo, heather, and some forms of spirea. The operation is performed by taking up plants and dividing them. This should be carried out in spring for foliage plants or those with late bloom, in autumn for those with early spring bloom, and at the beginning of growth in the spring for bamboo. The individual specimens are treated like young plants.

Shrubs with pliant branches, such as rhododendrons and magnolias, may be propagated by layering; that is, by bending a branch and pegging it into the ground after having girdled it slightly or after removing the bark. The tip of the shoot must be kept erect. With plants of long and very flexible branches, such as honeysuckle, each branch may go into and out of the earth several times, yielding more plants. Although this is a slow process (it may take two, three or more years before the offspring can be separated from the mother plant), it is a sure type of propagation, applicable to plants of particular value.

For air layering, moist sphagnum is placed around a girdled branch and wrapped with a piece of plastic. This ancient method, of Chinese origin, must have the medium kept constantly moist, which is easy when polyethylene is used. Production of roots is enhanced by the use of a rooting hormone on the surface of the branch before applying the sphagnum. Wind breakage is averted by fixing the package with splints. From the callus of the scar the roots emerge; when this occurs, the rooted branch is cut off and planted in a pot until the following spring. Spring is the most appropriate time of the year for air layering to obtain plants by early autumn. This is, however, a slow and laborious method, used especially for certain conifers and delicate shrubs.

Propagation by cuttings is the most common method of vegetative reproduction since the vegetative characteristics are reproduced. The method is economical as well, permitting an easy and rapid multiplication of a large quantity of plants. In the case of trees and shrubs, branches are usually placed in the medium for rooting; root cuttings are used of such genera as *Paulowia* and *Rhus.*

Cuttings may be of soft or green wood taken during summer, or of hard, mature wood taken in winter. Softwood cuttings are taken from June to September, from that year's growth; 2 to 6-inch pieces of branch are cut below a node, the lower leaves are removed, and the cuttings planted in sand, under glass, or in a humid greenhouse. The roots are formed when new growth is observed and the rooted cutting may then be transplanted. This method has a good success rate for most deciduous shrubs. Pines and such evergreens as *Aucuba,* camelia, oleander, box, privet, and euonymus are propagated in late summer, with partially mature wood.

Cuttings of hard, or mature wood, are made 6 to 12 inches long from the same year's growth, from November to February. They are sometimes taken with a "spur" of second year wood, which enhances rooting. They are placed in the sand with only one or two buds exposed. *Philadelphus, Deutzia, Forsythia, Spiraea, Tamarix, Cornus, Salix,* and various roses are propagated in this fashion.

Root cuttings are made of sections of roots and planted vertically in pots with the portion that was closest to the stem placed at the top. Rooting is improved by continuous mist.

Grafting is the intimate union of the tissues of two related plants, one of which has the root system (the stock) and the other, the graft (scion). For the scion a portion of a branch or a single leaf bud may be used; these are called, respectively, *grafting* and *budding.* These methods are used when cuttings take root with difficulty and with those plants whose characteristics do not come true from seed.

The practice is ancient; the Greeks knew budding, stem grafting, and crown grafting. The union of the two parts is effected by the two meristematic tissues, the *phellogen,* which produces bark on the outside and the cortical parenchyma on the inside, and the *cambium,* which generates the inner bark and the wood. It is necessary that stock and scion be related; the relationship is closest among varieties of the same species and between species of the same genus. Frequently, genera belonging to the same family (as between privet and lilac) may be grafted satisfactorily.

The cut must be smooth (use grafting knives that are well sharpened), and the surfaces must be clean. Besides the principal aim of propagation, grafting permits substituting one variety for another, growing a plant in soil not suited to it, obtaining greater vigour in the grafted plant, or dwarfing by the use of a weaker stock.

The forms of grafts are boundless, but those most used in gardening are: *approach grafts*, made by closely linking two stems after removing the bark at the point of contact—this is done for propagating mimosa; *cleft grafting*, done by shaping the scion like the mouthpiece of a flute and inserting it into a cleft of the stock; and *budding*, done by inserting a stem bud into a cut made T-shaped or in the form of a cross in the stock, the method used for garden roses.

Formerly, grafts were bound with raffia or wool thread; now there is widespread use of rubber bands, self-adhering gums, and adhesive tape. Bud grafts should be covered with mastic gum or dipped in paraffin to prevent drying and the growth of mould on the exposed surface.

The best time for budding is when the plant sap is most active; then the bark peels easily. Grafting is usually done towards the end of winter before plant growth begins. For slow-growing plants the union may take from 6 to 8 weeks. There are also types of root grafting: wisteria and rhododendrons are propagated in this way with ease; the union of stem and root occurs naturally.

Nursery operations

Plants obtained from seed or by vegetative reproduction, after having rooted, are "lined-out" in nursery beds with enough space for good development and root spread. Watering in the summer will be necessary, although it need be done only sparingly in the case of firs. One should not prune roots or branches of firs but they may be shortened in some broadleaved trees by removing one of the occasional double heads or encouraging a side branch to become the leader if the latter is gone. During this stay in the nursery, the development of the branches ("framework") begins that will in time produce a crown of foliage.

The best time for transplanting from the nursery is when the plant is dormant. Particular caution must be observed in the case of evergreens (especially firs), since they transpire uninterruptedly; one should therefore avoid periods of freezing or windy weather. To facilitate the transport of developed specimens of evergreens and firs, the ball of soil around the roots is usually wrapped in burlap.

Planting

As far as possible (especially in heavy soil) it is wise to till the soil well, months in advance, from 16 to 20 inches deep in what are to be permanent sites for trees so that frost, sun, and rain will make the soil loose and crumbly, permitting good circulation of air and water. In this operation subsoil, low in organic matter, should not be mixed with the topsoil.

When planting in poor soil, large holes are dug and replaced with good soil. Manure and peat can be incorporated. Wet soil should have a drainage layer of gravel at the bottom of the hole or a system of porous pipes to carry off water.

The quality and vigour of plants set out are related to their early growth; it is therefore important to make a wise choice of material for planting. Plants should have a trunk of good diameter and a balance between root system and top. It is preferable that the soil of the nursery bed and that of the permanent site be of a similar nature. The same may be said of the climate, although the climate of the nursery bed should be a little harsher, yielding hardier plants.

Holes should be large enough to allow a great deal of loose soil to be applied to the roots (5 to 6 feet wide and 3 feet deep). Autumn planting gives the best guarantee of success, except in the case of evergreens with a ball of earth which are planted in late winter, and palms which should be transplanted in June or July.

The roots must not be placed in contact with fertilizer. Suitable spacing is of great importance; this depends on the height the plant can attain, its habits (sun-loving or shade-loving), and the aesthetic effect sought. In digging holes for planting, it is better to keep subsoil separate from topsoil and to put the latter in contact with the roots. If immediate planting is not possible, the plants are "heeled in", with the roots in a trench and covered with earth. If plants have been partly frozen in transit, they must be thawed slowly in a sheltered spot; on the other hand, if the plants have been crowded close together in warm weather and overheated (by warmth generated through transpiration), they must be given air and moisture at once.

Plants should be set at the same depth they grow in the nursery. Burlap around the root ball should be loosely cut at the top, to free the roots, but not removed.

After planting it is almost always essential to keep the plant upright with a stake, in order to prevent it from being bent by winds and to keep the roots from being displaced. The stakes should be set parallel to the trunk, supporting it with elastic bands or metal wires covered with rubber to avoid injuring the bark. Slanting supports may be wires or poles.

Watering will be necessary immediately after planting. For large palms, water should be allowed to run from a hose for several days in succession at the base of the plant. Often the trunks are protected by metal grills, screen wire, thorny branches, etc., so they will not be displaced or damaged.

When very large specimens are to be transplanted, the root ball is made well ahead of time by digging a trench at some distance around the base of the tree and filling the trench with organic materials, such as peat moss. Transplanting can be done about six months later.

Digging and transporting trees are difficult procedures because of the risk of harming the branches or the bark,

10

especially with conifers. On the other hand, plane trees with a circumference of more than five feet, with all branches removed, may be planted in midsummer and then take good hold, forming a new top in a few years.

Culture

If there is a failure among trees planted for hedgerows or screens the gap should be filled as soon as possible. Larger trees may have to be used to keep pace with those already planted.

Care taken after planting consists of watering, cultivation, fertilizing, adjustment of the supports, trimming, and protection from cold and snow.

Cultivation consists of light hoeing of the layer of earth above the roots to break the crust that may be formed in tamping the soil. In the spring, chemical fertilizers are hoed shallowly into the earth. In both operations caution must be employed not to injure the roots, especially those of firs which grow new ones with difficulty. The binding of the supports must be inspected from time to time to make sure there is no danger of girdling the trunk.

Pruning may be needed to remove dead or diseased branches or suckers, to reinvigorate declining deciduous trees, to trim branches broken by snow or wind, to even the top, to increase height, to thin the trees (as, for example, when they are too close to electric power lines), and to shape screens and hedges. The cuts must be made with sharp tools flush with the trunk—without, however, damaging the bark.

There are many hindrances to free growth of street trees: trimming and other provisions made for the sake of safety (ensuring that the wind does not break off heavy branches, for example), the elimination of screens on public lighting, the danger of contact with overhead electric lines, too much shade, and the desire to give artificial shapes to the top.

Although pruning is needed especially by deciduous trees, it may be useful on certain conifers, such as Arizona cypress which if not trimmed loses its compact top, and boxwood and arborvitae when artificial shapes are wanted. The extent of pruning must be diversified according to the tolerance of the various kinds to this treatment.

If a given species does not tolerate drastic pruning, it is necessary to prune it lightly and more often. A particular and most specialized type of pruning is that by which so-called dwarf (or Bonsai) plants are achieved.

Pruning of flowering shrubs must be varied according to whether blooms appear on new growth or that of the preceding year. In the first case (as in *Philadelphus, Deutzia, Diervilla, Hydrangea*), in which flowering occurs in summer on new growth, pruning may be done until winter. In the second case one should wait until flowering is over (e.g., for *Forsythia* and *Jasminum nudiflorum*) so that new shoots for next year's bloom may then develop.

The most appropriate season for pruning is generally near end of winter, just before new vegetative growth begins. Evergreen species susceptible to frost should not be trimmed early, because their resistance to low temperatures is associated with the storing up of reserve substances that would be removed by pruning.

During heavy snows, especially if they are wet, broken branches of evergreens are avoided by shaking their tops and removing the weight of snow. Valuable or small plants are usually protected from cold, and especially from frost, with a protective covering of the trunk or of the entire plant, at least in their early years.

Prevention and cure of damage to trees

There are many causes of damage to trees; some of these, however, may be prevented. In case of construction near trees, they may be protected by a temporary fence, while in other cases adequate permanent defence can be provided to keep transient vehicles from coming too close (for example, in parking areas). Damage from cold (e.g., splitting from the action of frost) can be avoided by binding the trunks of delicate specimens with burlap. Specific insecticides will avoid or reduce the damage from insects.

When a branch is pruned, especially if it is large, the cut must be made properly without wounding the bark or leaving a stump. In any case, the cut must be smooth, clean, without rough edges, and slanted so that rainwater will run off. The cut surfaces are treated with preservatives such as asphalt paint or tar to prevent disease infection.

A frequent need in old specimens is the treatment of trunks hollowed by wood fungi, in general progressing from the bottom to the top. To restore strength to the weakened plant, it is first necessary to remove all of the decayed wood until live tissue is reached, then to disinfect and close the hole to keep other harmful organisms, that like humidity, from infesting it. The filling of large cavities is expensive and also very difficult because material with the same characteristics of expansion and contraction as wood do not exist. Mortar, cement, blocks of treated wood, mixtures of asphalt and sawdust, and magnesite are used for this purpose.

Large metal rings may be inserted in the cavity to reinforce the tree and to give better anchor to the filling material. The ring is kept in a narrow circumference relative to that of the trunk in order to permit it, if possible, to be filled with new tissue closing the wound. If there are only splits or soft wounds on the trunk, the edges of the wound are kept in place by metal clasps and a movable ring. These are also used, along with a metal stay rod, itself adjustable, to keep forked branches from growing further apart and splitting.

If the level of the terrain must be lowered, the level of that around the tree must be maintained by constructing a retaining wall. On the other hand, when the level of the terrain must be raised to ensure that the roots continue to be furnished with the normal amount of oxygen, the base of the tree must be kept free by creation of a well with dry walls around it. In addition a drainage layer of gravel, or, better still, porous drainage pipes set vertically and horizontally

A fungus harmful to woody plants: the honey mushroom (Armillariella mellea).

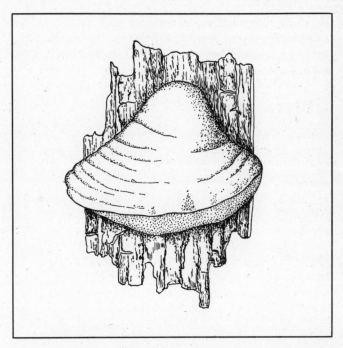

Another fungus that can cause the death of a tree; this appears as a flat surface or a clod attached to the trunk. Species of this sort are of the genera Fomes, Polyporus, Ganoderma, *etc.*

must be positioned beneath soil placed over the roots.

Lightning damage to trees does not usually occur when their whole surface is moist, since the discharge runs down along the trunk; but if the tree is struck at the beginning of a storm when the bark is still dry, the bark acts as an insulator, and the charge usually follows the cambium, killing it partially or entirely. Valuable specimens, especially if isolated and very tall, may be protected by lightning rods linked to the soil somewhat distant from the trunk.

Problems

The causes of damage or death to trees may be classified as climatic, human, insect, or due to diseases.

Climatic damage

Every plant has particular requirements in regard to its surroundings; if these are not respected, we may have plants that will grow with difficulty or not at all—or even die, in cases of extreme dryness, heat, or frost, for example. Often the great trees struck by lightning in parks lose their tops, are stripped of bark, or even die in the course of time.

Wet snowfalls or accumulations of freezing rain can split branches; strong winds can break branches or uproot the trees. Frost can cause longitudinal splits, leaving ugly calluses around the wound.

Cold air currents constantly from one direction may destroy the symmetry by partially drying up the top; near the sea, damage may be the result of salt spray.

Drought causes leaf-fall, drying of the branches, and in extreme cases death of the plant, which cannot substitute water absorbed for that lost by transpiration. And excess water deprives the roots of necessary oxygen and death results.

Human action

Very often it is man, directly or indirectly even if involuntarily, who causes damage to trees. We have already mentioned that "strangulation" by girdling and too close planting of trees causes deformation of the trunks and lack of symmetry in the crown.

Impenetrable street surfaces (asphalt or concrete) hinder the access of air and water to the roots. The harm from adding or removing earth at the foot of the tree has already been noted; also, excavations, drainage, and movement of earth in the vicinity can destroy the equilibrium of water supply by changing the level of the water table. Such conditions are unsatisfactory for root growth.

The air holds in suspension smoke, dust, and poisonous gases from domestic heating, from vehicular discharge, and from various industrial activities—all of which are damaging to trees. The air is most polluted where population is concentrated. The escape of gas underground has already been mentioned.

Insect attacks

Insect damage can affect any part of the plant; damage varies according to method of feeding, the biological cycle, and the degree of insect infestation.

Chewing insects cause defoliation. The several species of the winter moth group provide the majority of foliage-feeding caterpillars that move in a series of loops and so are known as "loopers". They feed upon apple trees, oak, hawthorn and beech. The moths emerge from the soil from

November to March, dependent on the species, and the wingless female ascends the tree on foot. The winged male seeks her out and after mating she lays eggs in crevices on twigs. When the caterpillars hatch out they feed mainly on the leaves but may also attack flowers and fruit.

Sucking insects nourish themselves on the sap inside the cells; aphids and scale insects are among the most harmful. The former sometimes cover the plants with downy or waxy efflorescence (e.g., the white aphids of the pine and the beech). The scale insects are covered with small shields and often envelop Japanese euonymus and other ornamentals.

These insects may be controlled by using insecticides. Since recommended controls change from time to time, specific materials will not be suggested in this book.

Old, declining trees are often attacked by wood-eating insects which dig out their passageways inside the bark. To this group belong also the white pine weevils (genus *Pissodes*) which cause desiccation of young shoots of conifers. The cypress poplar is host to numerous borers; the tunnels from which the sawdust comes out must be filled with a material that will give off poisonous vapours.

Leaf-mining insects disfigure leaves by tunnelling passages.

Diseases

The fungi harmful to the living parts of a plant are called parasites; because of their small dimensions they must be studied under a microscope. In some instances they belong to the group of ordinary mushrooms. Attacks of fungi cannot always be combated, especially if the affected plants are of great size.

In attempting to classify the pathogenic fungi according to their mode of action, those that cause the death of seedlings (plants that have just sprouted), such as damping-off organisms, are dealt with first. Other diseases attack the leaves, producing desiccation and leaf-fall; of this type are the black spots of maple leaves.

Mildew is caused by fungi that live on the surface of leaves, making them appear to be sprinkled with a whitish powder; various species live on oaks, roses, hydrangeas and lilacs.

Cankers are abnormal proliferation of cortical tissue, with swelling and malformation.

Rusts are so-called because the spores that issue from the tissues are rust-coloured. There are many species of fungi that attack various kinds of pines, and to complete their life cycle need the presence of certain herbaceous or shrubby plants (e.g., the currant, which is necessary for the complete life cycle of white pine rust).

A very serious vascular disease of the elm is the Dutch elm disease, caused by *Ceratostomella ulmi*; the pores of the tissues become occluded and the tree dries out. There is no remedy other than the substitution of an infected tree by the Siberian elm, which is immune. In most cases, the major damage to old trees in parks is due to root rot and core rot. Often the death of a tree already hollowed out is due to its weakness and the beating of the wind.

Now follows a description of trees and shrubs suitable and decorative for gardens. The trees are classified in sub-divisions of conifers and broadleaves, and the shrubs into flowering, leafy, and fruiting shrubs, according to the decorative effect of the bloom, the foliage or the fruit. For the genera or the families of plants with several species in use by horticulturalists, one among the representatives is completely described, with brief notes on other types worthy of interest. The list of plants has been arranged, as far as possible, in systematic order, although, in mentioning plants with related use, representatives of other families are sometimes included. Information on the morphology and cultivation of the species is also given.

Glossary

see illustration

*1. **Achene**—a dry, hard, indehiscent, single-seeded fruit with a single carpel.

2. **Acaulescent**—stemless

3. **Acuminate**—tapering to a point.

4. **Adnate**—united, grown together.

5. **Adventitious**—originating at other than the usual place; *roots* originating from any structure other than a root; *buds* arising from a part of the plant other than terminal or node.

6. **Alternate** (leaves)—one leaf at each node but alternating in direction.

7. **Annual**—a plant with a one-year life cycle.

8. **Anther**—that part of the stamen containing the pollen.

9. **Apetalous**—lacking petals.

10. **Apical**—terminal or summit.

11. **Axil**—the angle between a leaf and stem.

*12. **Berry**—a simple, fleshy fruit developed from a single ovule (loosely, any pulpy or juicy fruit).

13. **Biennial**—a plant with a two-year life cycle.

14. **Blade**—the expanded part of a leaf or leaflet.

*15. **Blossom**—the flower of a seed plant.

16. **Bract**—a specialized, modified leaf; of leaf-like structure.

17. **Bud**—a compressed stem; an underdeveloped stem.

18. **Bulb**—underground storage and reproductive organ with fleshy leaves called bulb scales.

19. **Calyx**—the outermost of the floral parts, composed of sepals.

*20. **Campanulate**—bell-shaped.

21. **Capitate**—shaped like a head.

*22. **Capsule**—a dry, dehiscent, multi-seeded fruit of more than one carpel.

23. **Carpel**—a leaf-like structure bearing ovules along the margins; a simple pistil.

*24. **Cauline**—related to an obvious stem or axis.

25. **Comose**—having tufts of hair.

*26. **Cordate**—heart-shaped.

27. **Corm**—an enlarged, underground stem, serving as a storage organ for food reserves.

28. **Corolla**—an inner cycle of floral organs, comprising the petals.

29. **Corymb**—a flat-topped, indeterminate flower cluster, with pedicels originating along a central peduncle; outer flowers open first.

30. **Cotyledons**—the first (seed) leaves of the embryo.

31. **Crenate**—toothed with rounded teeth.

32. **Crispate**—curled.

33. **Culm**—the stem of a grass or sedge.

34. **Cultivar**—a variety developed from known hybridization or origin.

35. **Cuneate**—triangular, wedge-shaped.

36. **Cyme**—a determinate flower cluster in which the central flower opens first.

37. **Deciduous**—plants that drop their leaves at the end of each season.

38. **Dehiscent**—opening of an anther or a fruit, permitting escape of pollen or seeds.

39. **Dentate**—toothed along the margins, apex sharp.

40. **Dichotomous**—divided into pairs; forked branches roughly equal.

41. **Dicotyledonous**—having two cotyledons.

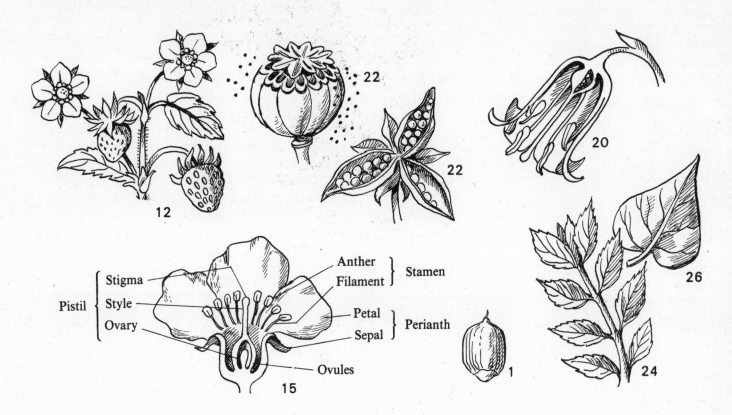

42. **Digitate** (leaves)—with leaflets arising from the apex of the petiole.

43. **Dioecious**—a species having male and female flowers on different, individual plants.

44. **Distichous**—in two vertical ranks, as the leaves of grasses.

*45. **Drupe**—a simple fleshy fruit, single carpel, with a hard endocarp containing the seed, e.g., the peach.

46. **Embryo**—a rudimentary plant.

47. **Entire**—without dentation or division.

48. **Epiphyte**—a plant that grows on another but is not parasitic.

49. **Fasciated**—an abnormally wide and flat stem.

50. **Filament**—the part of the stamen supporting the anther.

51. **Follicle**—a dry, dehiscent fruit with a single carpel, which dehisces along the ventral suture.

52. **Frond**—the leaf of a fern.

53. **Glabrous**—without hairs or pubescence.

54. **Glaucous**—covered with a whitish "bloom."

55. **Habit**—the general appearance of a plant.

*56. **Head**—a short, dense inflorescence, frequently with ray flowers around the margins and *tubular* disk flowers inside.

57. **Herbaceous**—non-woody.

58. **Hirsute**—hairy.

59. **Humus**—incompletely decomposed organic materials in the soil.

60. **Hybrid**—the result of a cross between two parents differing in genetic composition.

61. **Hydrophyte**—water loving; a plant adapted to wet conditions; capable of growing in water.

62. **Imbricate**—overlapping vertically or spirally.

63. **Indehiscent**—fruits remaining closed at maturity.

64. **Inflorescence**—the arrangement of flowers in a cluster; a complete flower cluster.

65. **Internode**—the part of a stem between two nodes.

66. **Involucre**—a cycle of bracts subtending a flower or an inflorescence.

67. **Keel**—the two front, united petals of most leguminous flowers, e.g., pea.

*68. **Lanceolate**—lance-shaped, narrow and tapered at the ends, widening above the base and narrowed to the apex.

*69. **Legume**—dry, dehiscent fruit, single carpel, usually opening along both sutures.

70. **Lenticils**—small, corky areas on woody stems.

71. **Lenticular**—lens-shaped.

72. **Ligulate**—strap-shaped.

73. **Ligule**—a thin membrane at the top of the leaf sheath in the grasses.

74. **Lip**—one portion of an unequally divided corolla; often of different sizes or colors as in orchids.

75. **Monoecious**—having male and female flowers on the same plant.

76. **Morphology**—form, structure, and development.

77. **Needle**—the long, narrow leaf characteristic of the conifers, as pine and spruce.

78. **Node**—point on a stem from which a leaf or branch emerges.

*79. **Opposite** (leaves)—two leaves at each node, opposite each other.

*80. **Palmate**—palm-like, radiating outward from the base.

*81. **Panicle**—a compound raceme.

*82. **Papilionaceous** (corolla)—a pea-like flower, having a standard keel and wings.

83. **Pedicel**—the stem of a single flower.

84. **Peduncle**—the stem of an inflorescence.

85. **Perrenial**—a plant that lives from year to year and does not die after fruiting.

86. **Perfect** (flower)—having both stamens and carpels in the same flower.

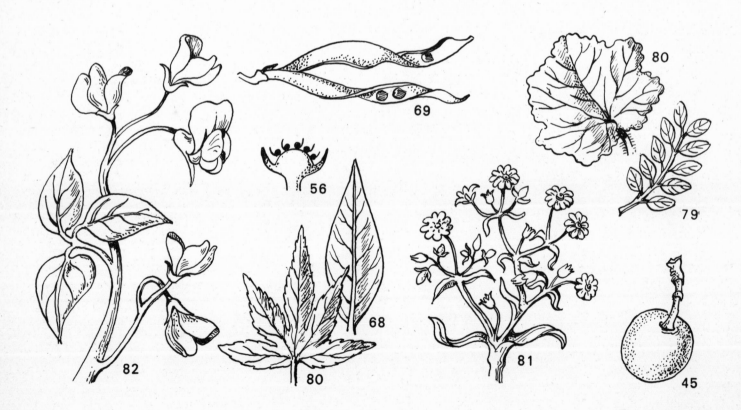

87. **Perianth**—the calyx and corolla.
88. **Persistent**—remaining attached.
89. **Petal**—one member of the corolla.
90. **Petiole**—the supporting stalk of the leaf blade.
91. **Pinnate**—separate leaflets arranged along a leaf stalk.
92. **Pistil**—the female reproductive parts of a flower, comprised of the stigma, style, and ovary.
*93. **Pome**—a fleshy, indehiscent fruit, with a leathery endocarp surrounding the seed, e.g., the apple.
94. **Pseudobulb**—thickened bulblike structure on leaves of epiphytic orchids.
95. **Pubescent**—covered with short hairs; downy.
96. **Raceme**—an elongated, indeterminate flower cluster with each floret on a pedicel.
97. **Rachis**—the axis of a spike.
98. **Receptacle**—the axis of a flower stalk bearing the floral parts.
99. **Reniform**—kidney-shaped.
100. **Reticulate**—as in a network of veins in a leaf.
101. **Rhizome**—an underground stem, usually horizontal, from which shoots and roots may develop.
102. **Rosette**—a cluster of leaves crowded on very short internodes.
103. **Rugose**—wrinkled.
104. **Sagittate**—arrow-shaped.
*105. **Samara**—a dry, indehiscent fruit having a wing, e.g., maple.
*106. **Scape**—a leafless flower stem arising from the soil.
107. **Schizocarp**—a dry, dehiscent fruit in which the carpels separate at maturation.
108. **Sepal**—a single member of the calyx.
109. **Septum**—a partition within an organ.
*110. **Serrate**—with sharp teeth and directed forward.

111. **Sessile**—without a stalk.
112. **Silique**—a dry, dehiscent fruit with two carpels separated by a septum.
113. **Sori**—spore masses on a fern.
*114. **Spadix**—a spike with a thick, fleshy axis, usually enveloped by a spathe.
*115. **Spathe**—a large bract or bracts surrounding an inflorescence.
116. **Spatulate**—spade-shaped; oblong with the basal end narrow.
*117. **Spike**—an inflorescence like a raceme except the florets are sessile to the peduncle.
118. **Stamen**—the male organ that bears the pollen.
119. **Standard** (in a papilionaceous corolla)—the large upper petal.
120. **Stigma**—the receptive part of the female organ.
121. **Stipule**—an appendage at the base of the petiole in some species.
122. **Stolon**—a prostrate stem that tends to root; sometimes called a runner.
123. **Style**—that part of the pistil connecting the stigma and the ovary.
124. **Succulent**—fleshy and juicy.
125. **Terrestrial**—plants growing in soil.
126. **Tomentose**—densely covered with hairs; woolly.
127. **Tuber**—underground storage organ; a stem with buds, e.g., the potato.
*128. **Umbel**—an indeterminate inflorescence in which the pedicels originate at about the same point on the peduncle and are about the same length, e.g., flowers of carrot.
*129. **Undulate**—a wavy surface.
130. **Variety**—a subdivision of a species, naturally occurring.
131. **Whorled**—leaves arranged in a circle around the stem.
132. **Wings**—(in a papilionaceous corolla)—the two side petals.
133. **Xerophyte**—a plant adapted to dry, arid conditions.

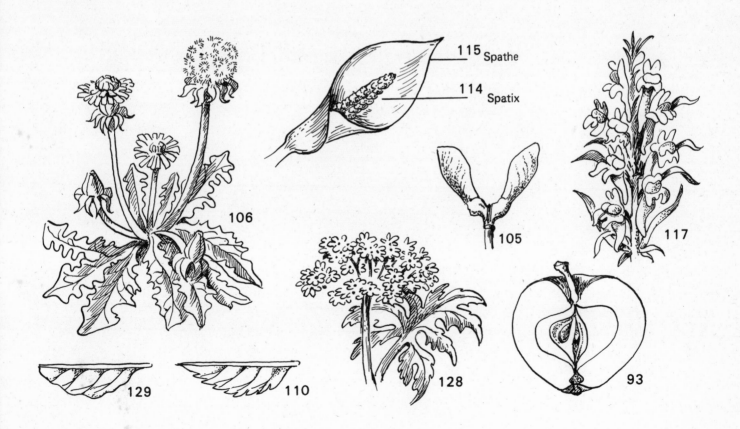

115 Spathe
114 Spatix
106
105
117
129
110
128
93

Index of plants mentioned

The conifers

Ginkgo

Ginkgo biloba (or Maidenhair tree) is sometimes listed in horticultural encyclopedias under the name *Salisburia adiantifolia* (family Ginkgoaceae). Although it is not a conifer, it has some similarities with such trees and for practical purposes is discussed with them.

The name of the genus is Chinese and signifies "trees with silver fruits". The two-lobed leaves give it its species name. Kaempfer discovered it in 1690 and published a description in 1712; in about 1730 the plant was grown for the first time in Europe in the Botanical Garden in Utrecht, and was introduced to Britain about 1750.

Morphology. It is a tall tree (60 to 120 feet), with a thick, erect trunk, few branches, a pyramidal top when young, later broadening, irregular, and always rather bare. The leaves are deciduous, fan-shaped with a notch at the tip, on a long pedicel, membranous and veined, light green, attached in groups of 3 to 5 to the short lateral branches set sparsely on the limbs. The bark is greyish, cracked, with rounded crests.

The male and female flowers are on separate plants; the male flowers are catkins and in clusters; the female are paired at the tip of a long peduncle (usually one of these aborts). The fruit is a drupe, fleshy, yellowish, and ill-smelling when ripe, whose ovoid seed has a thin shell.

Origin. This plant, botanically isolated from the monocots and dicots of the plant world, must be considered a living fossil, the sole representative of a group of plants that had their peak perhaps 200 million years ago.

Varieties. The varieties of the ginkgo are the following: *aurea*, with yellow leaves during the summer; *fastigiata*, with pyramidal habit; *laciniata*, with deeply-incised leaves; *pendula*, with weeping branches; *variegata*, with variegated-yellow leaves.

Cultivation. It is a hardy species, resistant to cold, liking deep, cool soil. It does not grow rapidly, but puts out long shoots at an early age.

This handsome tree can be planted in isolation or as a shade tree for streets in the south, or against south or west walls elsewhere. Plant only male trees to avoid the odour of the fruit. It is particularly picturesque in spring, when it puts out its beautiful, light-green leaves, and above all in autumn, when the top acquires a vivid golden colour. The wood has no use. The kernel of the seed, having a sweetish taste and being slightly resinous, is edible.

It is reproduced by seed (fertile only if trees of the two sexes are near each other), by cuttings, and by grafting. It is especially resistant to insects and diseases, and to air-pollutants, making it a good street tree in the south.

1. Specimen of *Ginkgo biloba* in autumnal colour.

2. Leaf and fruit.

3. Branch with the characteristic fan-shaped foliage.

2

3

4

5

6

7

8

9

Spanish fir

Abies Pinsapo, family Pinaceae
The name of this species derives from the Spanish dialect term for this tree.

Origin. It was introduced into European culture in 1838 by the botanist Boissier and met the immediate approval of landscape architects. In Britain specimens had been cultivated since the early seventeenth century.

Morphology. This is a tree of great height, which can surpass 75 feet, with a sturdy trunk, having many nodes and covered with dark grey bark, smooth on young trees, fissured on older specimens.

The top is pyramidal, rather broad, not very regular, with horizontal branches. The needles are short, thick, rigid, not very sharp, dark green, and the needles are set rather thickly all around the branch and more or less perpendicular to it.

The cones, lacking a peduncle, are erect, as in all the firs, and are brown or purple-brown, formed of numerous almost triangular scales, very broad and close together. The cone is persistent after seeds are shed.

Varieties. The principal horticultural species are the varieties: *aurea*, shrubby, with silver-grey needles; *glauca*, with glaucous needles; *hamondii*, dwarf, with a short trunk, broad branches spread out on the ground, and small needles.

Cultivation. This pine is an endemic species of the extreme southern tip of Spain. It lives in sparse forests, at altitudes of 3,500 to 6,000 feet, in areas heavily affected by grazing and by fires that hinder the renovation of flora. It is particularly adapted to a Mediterranean climate, and is tolerant to drought and low humidity; it is not tolerant to cold and is injured by temperatures below 5 degrees. It has no particular preference in soils, but does well on sandy loam.

The Spanish pine is a species of slow growth that has limited forest use. It is grown primarily as an ornamental tree.

Propagation is by seed, which is difficult to preserve and has a low level of germination. Seed is covered lightly in sowing; the shade-loving seedlings should be carefully protected from the sun and be kept moist. They may be propagated in the greenhouse by grafting, a terminal shoot being used as the scion; or a side shoot may be used as long as it is erect in growth.

Other species. Other species of fir are often grown in European parks. The Greek fir (*A. cephalonica*) has pungent foliage; it is a hardy species, resistant to summer drought, prefers full sun, suited to calcareous soil; it cannot stand a hard freeze. The Caucasian fir (A. *Nordmanniana*) has blunt needles, shiny on top, covering the branches thickly.

A. concolor, white fire, is native to the southwestern United States, has long, sparse needles, silver-grey on both sides. *A. balsamea* is a favourite species for Christmas trees (Balsam fir), and *A. lasiocarpa* is the Rocky Mountain Fir.

10

11

13

15

Douglas fir

Pseudotsuga taxifolia or *P. Douglasii*, family Pinaceae

The term *Pseudotsuga* means "false Tsuga" because of the resemblance of their needles to those of hemlock; *taxifolia* means "with foliage like yew".

Origin. This magnificent tree was discovered by Archibald Menzies on Vancouver Island in 1795 and introduced by David Douglas to Great Britain in about 1826.

Morphology. The Douglas fir reaches 200 to 300 feet, placing it among the taller trees. When young, its bark is grey and smooth, dotted, however, with small blisters full of resin resembling cedar in aroma; later the bark splits, becoming corky, and one may observe two kinds of secondary bark, one of plates and another with deep longitudinal, sparse cracks.

The habit of isolated trees is pyramidal, with a long, regular, pointed top; the branches are in somewhat regular whorls, the upper ones horizontal, the lower ones bending downwards.

The needles are attached to the branches at right angles, like teeth of a comb; they are linear, flat, soft, green, marked on the lower side with two blue-green lines of stomata.

The cones are easily differentiated from those of other conifers; they are ovoid, reddish brown, with woody scales that are thin, rounded or convex, alternate, with longer trilobed bracts, and with a sharply pointed central lobe.

Varieties. Species thriving in the wild in western portions of North America, from British Columbia to Mexico, include: var. *menziesii*, (green or Oregon Douglas fir); var. *glauca* with smaller leaves and cones; and var. *caesia*, leaves bluish green and intermediate between the two preceding in morphology and ecology.

The variety *glauca*, commonly known as the blue or Colorado Douglas fir, is a handsome ornamental tree, not as tall, with intensely blue-green foliage and similar bracts of cones, turned up, however, when ripe, and a longer central lobe; this variety is more resistant to dry climates and to frost than is the green Douglas fir.

Other horticultural varieties include *fastigiata*, *pendula*, *brevibracteata*, *argentea* (with silver-white leaves), *aurea* (leaves at first light yellow), and *Fretsii* (leaves short and broad).

Cultivation. In general the green Douglas fir needs acid, deep, fertile, and well-drained soil and a humid, maritime climate; its resistance to frost and late cold spells is related to the production of seed. When young, it grows best in light shade; later it becomes sun-loving. It may suffer from strong winds, but thrives on abundant rainfall.

The wood is valued for many uses, including building, railway sleepers, and masts; its warm, reddish colour and regular, fine veining are prized for plywood.

This long-lived and fast-growing plant is re-

produced by seed sown 1 inch deep in open beds during March, and transplanting the seedlings when two years old. The horticultural varieties are propagated by grafting.

One of the most common diseases to afflict this tree is caused by a fungus, *Phomopsis pseudotsugae*, which causes several types of damage. The leading and lateral shoots die back to about 12 inches, with leaves going brown and yellow and quickly falling off. Cuts on the bark may be affected and this in time leads to girdling. Another fairly common ailment is known as resin bleeding. At the base of the branches and on lesions in the main trunk there is a profuse resin exudation. This condition is probably caused by several types of fungi.

---

4. *Abies cephalonica.*

5, 8. *Abies concolour* and detail.

6. *Abies Nordmanniana* and its cone.

7, 9. Details of *Abies Pinsapo.*

10, 11. Branches with young cones of *Pseudotsuga taxifolia* var. *glauca* and var. *viridis.*

12. *Pseudotsuga taxifolia* and its cone.

13. Female flower of the same plant.

14. View of the trunk of an old specimen of *P. taxifolia.*

15. Branch of the same species.

16

17

18

19

20

21

Colorado spruce

Picea pungens, family Pinaceae
The name of this genus was already in use among the Romans, who derived it from *pix,* referring to the pitch; the ending *pungens* is due to the aromatic foliage.

Morphology. This is a tree that may reach 150 feet; it has a brownish-grey bark deeply cracked and scaly in old specimens; the top is narrowly pyramidal, quite regular in shape if grown in the open.

The needles are solitary, linear, rigid, incurved, sharp and blue-green, attached all around the twig, which is light orange-brown.

The cones are pendulous, cylindrical, light brown and shiny at maturity, with soft scales that are blunt at the top, toothed and wavy.

Varieties. The variety most cultivated, for its silvery blue-green foliage, is the *Kosteriana,* with pendulous branches; there are also the varieties *argentea, viridis, aurea, flavescens, prostrata,* and *tabuliformis.*

Cultivation. It is a plant of high altitudes in the Rocky Mountains, from Montana to New Mexico, where it grows at 5,500 to 10,000 feet. It is a hardy species, resistant to cold and to drought; it grows best where summers are cool and winters severe. It prefers full sun and tolerates wind and the polluted air of cities. The bluish forms are more delicate and can lose their original colour or even their needles from aphid infestation when planted in a mild climate. This spruce grows rather slowly and is long-lived.

This tree is frequently used ornamentally in gardens; if specimens with a more specialized appearance are desired, *Kosteriana* will make handsome spots of colour. Propagation in nature is by seed; cultivars are propagated by grafting.

Other species. Some other species of the genus *Picea* are cultivated as ornamentals, including the Common or Norway spruce (*Picea Abies*), the traditional Christmas tree. A forest plant of mountains and foothills, resistant to extremes of weather, this tree is suited to planting in any soil, provided that the winters are cold and summers not too dry. Because of its shallow root system it may be uprooted by strong winds. It will not tolerate heavy air pollution. At low altitudes, young specimens are often attacked by an aphid. Its timber is known as white deal.

A dwarf form of the Common spruce is *P. Ellwangeriana,* and a weeping variety is *P. pendula. P. Gregoryana,* a very dwarf form and conical, grows to 2 feet.

The Serbian spruce is similar (*Picea Omorika*). The Oriental spruce is rather elegant (*P. orientalis*), and is found throughout Turkey and the Caucasus. It has a regular, pyramidal top, its dense branching down to the ground, and its short-needled foliage. The cones are small.

16, 17, 19. *Picea pungens* and its twigs.

18. *Picea pungens* var. *Kosteriana.*

20. *Picea Abies.*

21. *Picea Abies* var. *pendula.*

22

23

Atlas cedar

Cedrus atlantica, family Pinaceae
The name of the genus derives from the Greek *kedros*; the species name indicates its origin, the Atlas chain of mountains in Morocco.

Morphology. The trunk is thick and strong; the branches, frequently ascending; the top, broad, but sparse; the habit, pyramidal with an erect terminal shoot when young, in old specimens assuming flat layers. It can attain a height of 100 to 125 feet. The needles are short, stiff, sharp, and rectangular; they are sparse on new growth and attached in spirals on small lateral branches.

The cones are rather large, erect, bottle-shaped, resinous with membranous scales that are short and wide, closely shingled, of a violet purple colour before ripening. The bark is grey and smooth in young specimens, but later develops into brown scales.

Varieties. The variety most known and widespread is *glauca* with blue-grey needles. *Argenta* has grey-blue foliage, and *aurea* golden foliage.

Origin. It is native to the Atlas mountains of Morocco and some Algerian mountains at 5,500 to 7,000 feet, in humid to semi-dry climates.

Cultivation. It requires a well-drained soil and ample space, preferring full sun. It tolerates dry summers and severe cold as low as −25°C (−10°F).

It is an important plant in its country of origin and is used for reforestation in sub-Mediterranea zones. It does particularly well in seaside areas. In gardens it is employed in isolated groups on expanses of lawn; to form a handsome colour contrast, the variety *glauca* may be used. It is propagated by seed, by cuttings, or by grafting. The fall of needles in winter in urban areas is blamed on smog.

Other species. *Cedrus Deodara*, the Deodar cedar has longer needles of a slightly bluish green and a curved top. The oldest cedar in England at Brethby Park, Derbyshire, planted in 1676, is a Cedar of Lebanon, *C. libani*; in old specimens this has a decidedly flattened top.

24

22. *Cedrus atlantica.*

23, 24. *Cedrus atlantica* var. *glauca*, and detail.

25. *Cedrus Deodara.*

26. *Cedrus libani* (Cedar of Lebanon).

25

26

27

28

29

30

31

Pine

Genus *Pinus*, family Pinaceae
The major description here is of *Pinus nepalensis*, the Himalaya white pine, otherwise known as *Pinus griffithii*.

Morphology. *P. nepalensis* is a pine with elegant habit, characterized by great height (100 feet in cultivation, 170 in nature), a rather rigid top, shaped in a pyramid, with branches more or less horizontal, arching a little upwards at the ends, regularly whorled and with abundant needles that are long and thin, bluish-green, soft, pendant, and clustered in groups of five.

The cones are about 10 inches long, cylindrical, attenuated at both ends, resinous, formed of oval scales with a thick spatulate tip that opens wide at maturity. The timber reaches maturity at about 80 years.

Varieties. There are two varieties, not often cultivated, *monophylla*, with isolated needles, and *zebrina*, with needles striped green and yellow. Hybrid forms of this plant with *P. Strobus* are known in cultivation, characterized by shorter and not so weeping needles, as are hybrids with *P. Ayacahuite*. The latter have less resistance to cold, being native to Mexico. These hybrids are usually the result of planting seeds gathered from trees in parks where cross-fertilization is enhanced.

Origin. The *P. nepalensis* is a native of the Himalayan forests from 5,500 and 13,000 feet up, and from Afghanistan to Nepal.

Cultivation. In culture it behaves as in the wild—resistant to cold, adapted to gravelly or sandy soils. It prefers a humid climate and is somewhat resistant to air pollutants; it grows rapidly but has a short life in cultivation.

It is frequently used in parks and gardens and occasionally as a street tree.

In timber-producing countries *P. nepalensis* is often planted for its soft, light wood, which is used for woodworking and paper pulp.

This tree is more resistant to blister rust and air pollution than other white pines.

Other species. Many other pines are grown as ornamentals: the white pine (*Pinus Strobus*) is a close relative of *P. nepalensis*, and is a native of North America, from the Great Lakes to the Appalachians. It is distinguished by shorter needles, in erect brushes, and cones smaller (about 4 inches) although otherwise similar. It is an excellent ornamental that becomes most attractive later than *P. nepalensis* because its rapid growth and shorter needles leave a sparse top when young. It is also planted in countries with good summer rainfall and cold winters, to produce lumber for woodworking and for paper pulp. The tree is attacked by blister rust, which causes cankers and the death of the plant.

In hillside gardens the Swiss Stone Pine (*P. Cembra*) makes a good effect. The species is slow-growing, and has clusters of five needles. In the Mediterranean region, the Italian Stone Pine, *P. Pinea*, is a principal element of the landscape, with its characteristic umbrella-shaped top and paired needles.

The pine often used in more difficult situations

32

33

34

Giant sequoia

Sequoiadendron giganteum, family Taxodiaceae. The name of the genus means tree (from the Greek *dendron*) of Sequoia, a Cherokee Indian of the United States of the eighteenth century who invented the Cherokee alphabet.

This splendid tree was discovered by David Douglas in 1831 and introduced into Great Britain by Lobb in 1854. Douglas, a famous plant hunter, was gored to death by a bull while on an expedition.

Morphology. The sequoia is the giant of plants, reaching 300 feet or more in the natural state, with an enormous circumference (e.g. 100 feet, in the specimen called General Sherman).

The species has exceptional longevity (perhaps beyond 3,000 years), which puts it in second place among the most ancient living beings (the first is held by specimens of Bristle-Cone Pine *Pinus aristata* of the Rocky Mountains, more than 4,600 years old).

The trunk is massive, narrowly pyramidal, enlarged at the base, characterized by a very thick, fibrous, spongy base with deep and longitudinal cracks. The top is dense, typically conical, and close-packed, formed of branches bending towards the lower parts.

The needles are small, alternate, scale-shaped, imbricate (edged like tiles), covering the twigs.

The cone is ovoid, formed of wedge-shaped scales with a furrowed, rhomboid tip.

The tree is susceptible to the fungus *Botrytis cinerea*, or grey mould.

Varieties. Some varieties are known: *aureum*, *glaucum*, and *pendulum*.

Origin. The giant sequoia originates from a limited area of California (the Sierra Nevadas) at from 5,000 to 8,000 feet, in a temperate climate with abundant snowfall.

Cultivation. In culture this tree needs deep loam and prefers areas with damp climate and air. It tolerates winter cold and shade quite well. Because of the dimensions it reaches, it is suited to planting as a single specimen in large parks and for forming majestic lanes.

It is reproduced by seed, by cuttings, or by grafting; it re-sprouts easily from stumps which is rare among conifers.

Other species. *Sequoia sempervirens*, the Redwood, also cultivated, is a tree that can attain similar heights, although smaller in diameter. It has flat, almost comb-like needles about one inch long and mostly in two ranks.

It originates from the costal areas of northern California and needs high summer humidity and winters that are not too severe. It grows rapidly, and it is long-lived. It was introduced into Britain in the mid-nineteenth century.

(heavy, dry, calcareous soil) is the Austrian pine (*P. nigra*), which exists in several forms and is a good shelter tree.

For rock gardens and for sustaining terraces is the dwarf Mugo pine (*P. Mugo* var. *Mughus*), with prostrate, globose form, of Central European origin. A dwarf form suitable for rockeries is *P. Watereri*.

27. *Pinus nepalensis*, Himalaya White Pine.

28. *Pinus Strobus*, white pine.

29. *Pinus Pinea*, Italian Stone Pine.

30. *Pinus nigra*, Austrian Pine.

31. *Pinus Mugo* var. *Mughus*, dwarf Mugo pine.

32. Trunk of *Sequoiadendron giganteum*.

33, 34. *Sequoia sempervirens* and detail.

35

38

36

39

37

40

Bald cypress

Taxodium distichum, family Taxodiaceae
The name of the genus refers to a similarity of the needles of those of the yew (*Taxus*); *distichum* means "in a double row", referring to the arrangement of the needles on the twigs. It is sometimes known as the swamp cypress.

Morphology. It is a large tree with deciduous foliage (an exception among conifers), 100 to 135 feet tall, with a top somewhat irregular when old. The trunk is straight, thick at the base, and it has a rather thin bark, which is reddish-brown, fibrous, and scaly. In swampy soil with poor soil aeration the peculiar cypress knees grow vertically from the roots; their purpose is to bring air to the roots when the soil is covered with water.

The needles are linear, herbaceous, light green, whitish underneath, set like the teeth of a comb in the sides of the twigs, which drop with them in the autumn.

The cones are almost spherical, reddish, woody or cork-like, rough, and terminate in a hard, short point.

The variety *pendens* has drooping branches.

Origin. The bald cypress is native to the coasts and rivers of the southern United States, where it grows in flooded or swampy zones, although in cultivation it adapts well to dry soil.

Cultivation. Although it comes from a temperate or warm-temperate climate, it is resistant to cold, except for young plants. In Britain the bald cypress does well on lawns in a sheltered position where there is plenty of sun. It is used in parks, especially near water, where it makes its greatest growth, and so does well in soil with poor drainage. Its foliage is very colourful in autumn, becoming a rusty red. Propagation is by seed or cuttings.

Other species. To the same family belongs another decorative conifer, *Cryptomeria japonica*, native to Japan and China, evergreen, with awl-shaped needles and a serated and conical top; in old specimens the straight trunk has a handsome reddish-brown bark that sheds. It is recommended for cool but not too cold climates. The variety *elegans* is especially appreciated for its fine foliage and its rusty-red colour in winter. It is low growing. Besides propagation by seed, *Cryptomeria* may be propagated by cuttings or air layering.

Another tree of this family, the Umbrella Pine (*Sciadopitys verticillata*), is evergreen, usually 50 to 60 feet tall, and has a rather thin top. Some of the leaves are scaly and some are long, arranged in whorls. Cultural requirements are similar to cryptomeria but this slow-growing tree is more resistant to cold, even so it should be sheltered from piercing winds.

35, 36. *Taxodium distichum* and detail of its trunk and branches.

37. Twig with cones of *Taxodium distichum*.

38. *Cryptomeria japonica*.

39, 40. *Sciadopitys verticillata* and detail.

41

Italian cypress

Cupressus sempervirens var. *stricta*, family
Cupressaceae

The early Romans used this plant and gave it
its name "*sempervirens*", meaning evergreen. It
has been cultivated since ancient times and has
featured in much romantic poetry and prose
typified by Lord Byron who wrote in *The Bride
of Abydos*:

Know ye the land where the cypress and myrtle
Are emblems of deeds that are done in their
  clime;
Where the rage of the vulture, the love of the
  turtle,
Now melt into sorrow, now madden to crime?

To the Romans the Italian cypress was a tree
of death, probably for two reasons. As the tree
grows old its foliage blackens, and once it is cut
down it rarely grows again. The tree is often
grown in cemeteries, even in Britain although
the climate here is not suited to it.

In the past it was used for boat building—
Alexander the Great used it to build his fleet.

Morphology. In the description of this tree, the
var. *stricta*, commonly used as an ornamental, is
referred to first, and then follows the diverse
characteristics of another variety *horizontalis*.
The Italian cypress is a tall tree (up to 100 feet),
with a trunk which is not always circular in
cross-section but exhibits, especially at the base,
buttresses and ribbing, and is covered with a
bark finely but not deeply cracked longitudinally,
grey-brown, and fibrous. The top is typically
compact, columnar or spindle-shaped, formed of
abundant, erect branches with twigs completely
covered by minute, scale-like, oval-obtuse
needles, which are close together and dark
green. The cones are spherical with woody scales.

Varieties. *C. sempervirens* var. *horizontalis*,
has horizontal branches; the top is less dense and
the tree has a pyramidal habit. It is sometimes

used as the first step in reforestation and does
well in groups as a windbreak.

Origin. Although widespread, the cypress
exists today only under cultivation; it is believed
to have originated in the eastern basin of the
Mediterranean, from which it was distributed for
ornamental use.

Cultivation. The cypress is a xerophile (tolerating drought) and quite a hardy tree, suited to
poor, stony soils. It will not flourish in wet soil
and prefers mild winters. Moderately shade-
loving, it is among the most long-lived trees; in
Italy, specimens many centuries old are known.

This is the classic cypress of Tuscan and
Umbrian districts of Italy. It is grown as an individual tree, and in southern Europe in rows for
street plantings. It may be pruned to make
hedges and screens. The wood resists insect
damage and is used for furniture and in building.

Propagation is by seed; the young plants have
difficulty becoming established if transplanted
with bare roots, so seed is sown in containers and
seedlings are transplanted with the ball of earth.

Other species. The Arizona cypress (*Cupressus
arizonica*) is resistant to cold and has a tapering
top. It is usually pruned so that it remains dense
and full.

A species native to California is *C. macrocarpa*.
Monterey Cypress, with a dense, broad top.
Variety *lutea* has yellow leaves when young.

---

41. Group of Italian cypresses (*Cupressus sempervirens* var. *stricta*).

42. Detail of the top of the same species.

43. *Cupressus arizonica*. Arizona cypress.

44. *Cupressus macrocarpa*, Monterey cypress.

42

43

44

45

47

48

False-cypress

Chamaecyparis Lawsoniana, family Cupressaceae
This plant (the name in Greek means "small cypress") is called Lawson's cypress. Despite its common name, the genus is only related to the true cypress. *Chamaecyparis nootkatensis* will hybridize with *Cupressus macrocarpa*, however.

Morphology. This tree is very tall in the wild (up to 160 feet); in cultivation it does not reach this height and is sometimes dwarf. The shape is conical, the head dense, the bark brown and deeply fissured longitudinally. The small, scale-like leaves completely cover the branchlets in four rows, the branchlets are opposite, giving the branches a frond-like appearance. The cone is small.

Varieties. The varieties are numerous and are distinguished by the foliage colouration, those with a columnar habit (some with pendant branches), those with a spreading habit, and the dwarfs.
  Among the foliage variants are the following: *albospica* (compact top, branchlets creamy white at the top); *argentea* (foliage silvery); *aurea* (golden yellow); *glauca* (leaves steel-blue); *lutea* (young growth bright yellow).
  Among the columnar varieties are *Allumii* (with blue-green needles), *erecta*, *Fletcheri* (with awl-shaped needles when young), *Pottersii* (with needles of mixed types), and *pyramidalis alba* (with branch tips white in spring). The variety *filiformis* is one of the weeping types.
  Varieties with a spreading habit include:

gracilis, *lycopodioides*, and others. Among small, slow-growing varieties there are *nana*, a globose, bright-green shrub, and *nana* f. *glauca*.

Origin. The Lawson cypress is native to the western United States, along the Pacific coast (Oregon and California). Rainfall is high and the summers are dry, although the air is humid.

Cultivation. It grows on many types of soils if deep, fertile, and well-drained. It is not harmed by cold and will tolerate shade. It is frequently used in closely-spaced groups because of its slender habit; a collection of varieties produces a good effect. It may also be used for hedging and screens. The typical Lawson cypress is reproduced by seed and the varieties from cuttings.

Other species. Two other species are frequently planted: the Hinoki cypress, *C. obtusa*, often variety *nana*; and Sawara cypress, *C. pisifera*, with varieties *filifera* and *filifera aurea*. To the same family belongs the incense-cedar (*Libocedrus decurrens*), somewhat resembling the Lawson cypress, with needles hanging from the twigs.

---

45. *Chamaecyparis Lawsoniana*, variety *globosa*.

46. *C. Lawsoniana* variety *aurea*.

47. Group of *Chamaecyparis Lawsonia*.

48. Detail of the cultivar Golden King.

46

Yews

Taxus baccata, family Taxaceae

The name of the genus was in use among the Romans; *baccata* means "berry-producing". This species is the Common yew. Due to its sombre appearance it is often seen in cemeteries and churchyards, and many poets have used its association with death.

Morphology. It is an evergreen, 30–50 feet tall, generally with more than one trunk, irregular in form with numerous broad, ascending branches supporting a wide, dense, concave top. The bark is reddish-brown, thin, and scale-like.

The leaves, similar to pine needles, are linear, flattened, sickle-shaped, dark green, pointed, attached to the twigs like a comb.

The plant is dioecious. Fruit on the female specimens at the end of summer are berry-like, red, open at the end. The seed and the foliage are poisonous.

Varieties. The botanical varieties are numerous and include: *adpressa* (with short, oval-oblong needles and low habit), *aurea*, *compacta*, *erecta*, *glauca*, *horizontalis*, *nana*, *procumbens*, and *stricta*.

Origin. This species is native to Europe and Northern Asia, near the coasts, but its numbers have been reduced because of the value of the wood for cabinet making or because the foliage is poisonous to livestock.

Cultivation. It prefers deep, fertile soil, but will also thrive in fissured, rocky soil; it requires good drainage. It tolerates cold and has great longevity (more than 1,000 years).

Used as isolated specimens and for hedges, it is easy to shape by pruning and is a favourite tree for clipping for topiary work, and is one of the trees used in the famous maze at Hampton Court Palace. It may be planted under tall trees and in northern exposures.

The wood is durable with a very fine grain, and with polish takes on a brilliant surface, so is used in veneers, inlays, and cabinet work. Reproduction of the species is by seed; the varieties are propagated by layering or cuttings in the greenhouse during summer or by grafting in spring on potted rootstock. Cuttings grow slowly and often remain shrubby.

Other species. The plum-yew, *Cephalotaxus Fortunei*, resembles yew although belonging to another family, Cephalotaxaceae, and is a tall shrub with many, pendant branches. The needles have two glaucous lines underneath and are somewhat longer. The fruit is the size and shape of an olive and brownish when ripe. It originated in China and is grown as an ornamental. It has several varieties. The Japanese Yew, *T. cuspidata* grows to 50 feet.

---

49. *Chamaecyparis obtusa* var. *gracilis*.

50. *Chamaecyparis pisifera* var. *filifera*.

51. Twig of *Taxus baccata*, with fruit.

52. *Taxus baccata* var. *stricta*.

53. Detail of *Cephalotaxus Fortunei* twig.

49

50

51

52

53

Monkey puzzle

Araucaria araucana = A. imbricata, family Araucariaceae

The name of the genus and species is from its country of origin, southern Chile, where the native people were called Araucans; the name imbricata is from the scale-like structure of the needles.

The plant was discovered about 1780 and introduced into Europe by Archibald Menzies in 1795, although for many years it continued to be a rarity. Menzies sailed with Captain Vancouver on voyages that took them along the coast of Chile, and it was from here that the botanist collected seeds of the monkey puzzle tree. Some of the plants grown from this seed were presented to the Royal Botanic Gardens at Kew. The last one died nearly a century later in 1892.

Morphology. This tree may reach 130 feet; the columnar trunk is usually branched to the ground. In old trees a secondary bark with platelets is formed; the trunk, after losing its needles, remains for many years marked by their scars. The limbs are in whorls of 4 to 9, horizontal or inclined downwards in the lower part and somewhat upturned at the top; they are completely covered with thick, leathery, oval or lanceolate, pointed needles, which remain alive for 10 to 15 years and still persist when they become dry.

The monkey puzzle tree has male and female plants. The fruit is large, spherical-ovoid, formed of numerous wedge-shaped, lanceolate scales with a long point, leathery and woody; they do not always contain fertile seeds. The seeds are large, shiny and edible.

Varieties. Although not widespread, some varieties of this plant exist: *platifolia* has rather broad needles; *striata*, with trunk and needles striped yellow; *aurea*, with golden yellow needles.

Cultivation. The monkey puzzle lives in a temperate climate with winter snow and abundant rainfall, usually in hardwood forests. It prefers a moist, well-drained, acid soil. It does not tolerate rapid drops in temperature and needs a high, dry, and sheltered position not exposed to industrial smoke.

In view of its peculiar habit, this tree is best used in a single specimen or in small groups. But it can be mixed with other trees in a sheltered position, particularly where winters are harsh, to prevent dehydration of the branches and the resultant destruction of the symmetry that is the principal charm of the plant.

The monkey puzzle has no commercial use in Britain but produces valued timber in Chile, where at one time it was used in shipbuilding.

Araucaria is propagated by seed or by cuttings, a terminal shoot being used. There are also a number of greenhouse species originating in Australasia.

Other species. Another hardy species is *Araucaria araucana* var. *aurea*, with golden-tinted foliage.

---

54. *Araucaria araucana*, monkey puzzle tree.

Broadleaved trees

Black walnut

Juglans nigra, family Juglandaceae
Juglans is the ancient Latin name for the walnut; *nigra* refers to the dark colour of the bark. It was first grown in Britain about 1585.

Morphology. This is a tall tree, reaching 100 to 150 feet. The trunk is blackish, fissured at an early age. The tree has a broad crown, and is oval or rounded in form. The leaves are large, alternate, deciduous, odd-pinnate with numerous oval-lanceolate pointed, toothed leaflets, hairy beneath along the vein.

The plants are monoecious, the male flowers are green catkins, the females are single or clustered, with a small corolla and two short styles. The fruit is globose and contains a furrowed nut in a fleshy, yellowish-green epicarp with a pebbled, downy surface.

The nut is rough and hard and contains a tasty kernel. It is rather difficult to remove from the shell and thin-shelled types are sought.

Varieties. This tree varies little, but some horticultural varieties are grown.

Origin. The black walnut is native to eastern U.S., from Massachusetts to Florida and Texas. It was introduced into Britain in the late sixteenth century.

55

Cultivation. It does not tolerate crowding and dense shade, and is usually planted as a single tree in town gardens; it prefers a deep soil that is fertile and moderately moist but well-drained. In good soil it grows more rapidly, and lives up to 250 years.

In parks it is used as a specimen tree or in lanes; it needs adequate space.

The wood is used for furniture, panelling and gun stocks. The heart wood is dark-brown; the sapwood is whitish.

Propagation is by planting the mature nuts in the autumn. Viability is short-lived since, being rich in oil, the nuts easily become rancid; they may be preserved during winter in cool sand and sown $1\frac{1}{2}$ to 2 inches deep the following spring. Light soil is preferred because the plant produces a long tap root in heavy soil making transplanting after one or two years usually quite difficult. The black walnut is rarely attacked by insects.

Other species. Another ornamental Juglandaceae is *Pterocarya fraxinifolia*, the Caucasian Wing-Nut, also with compound leaves, many leaflets, and a pendant inflorescence. *J. regia*, found from the Caucasus to the Himalayas, grows to 60 feet, and *J. cinera*, the Butter Nut, of similar height is native to North America.

55. Fruiting branches of *Juglans nigra*.

56. Branches of *Pterocarya fraxinifolia*, with inflorescence.

57

58

59

Weeping willow

Salix babylonica, family Salicaceae
Salix is the Latin word for willow. The species name suggests Babylonia as the place of origin of the tree, although in reality it is native to China and Manchuria, from which it was introduced into Europe about 1730.

Napoleon was an admirer of the tree and one was planted by his tomb at St Helena. This died and more were planted to replace it.

Morphology. The tree is of small stature, reaching 30 to 40 feet, with a very broad crown; the limbs are spreading and bear numerous slender branches of a purplish or olive-green colour, which are drooping, giving the tree its common name.

Leaves are alternate, deciduous, narrow-lanceolate to lanceolate, pointed, on a short petiole, with minutely toothed edges. They are smooth, often bluish-green underneath.

The plant is dioecious and the flowers appear in spring along with the foliage. The flowers are soft catkins; the males are yellow, the females green. Fruits have white, cottony hairs and are carried by the wind. Female trees of the willow outnumber the male.

Varieties. A very distinct variety is *crispa*, in which the leaves are twisted to form a ring. Variety *aurea* has golden branches. Also in cultivation are *S. sepulcralis* and *S. blanda*, hybrids of *S. babylonica* with *S. alba* and *S. fragilis*, respectively. Propagation is by cuttings of shoots or stems in moist soil in October.

60

61

Lombardy poplar

Cultivation. Weeping willow requires moist or at least cool soil. It is much used as an isolated specimen in gardens, mirrored in lakes or streams, but too often it is incongruously mixed with plants of different form. The wood, soft, light and brittle, has no practical value.

It propagates with ease from cuttings which need no particular care.

The major damage to willows comes from infestations by defoliating and boring insects. The tree is subject to breakage in high winds.

Other species. Other willows to use in moist, sandy soil that are ornamental in winter are the Purple Osier, *S. purpurea*, with branches of a brilliant purple colour, and *S. alba* var. *vitellina*, with yellow branches. *S. alba* var. *calva* is used for making cricket bats. *S. Caprea* supplies wood for scythe and rake handles, hoops, poles and crates.

S. Matsudana var. *tortuosa* is a relatively recent introduction from China, where it is called Lung Chao Liu, curious in having twisted branches and curled leaves. It is sometimes called corkscrew willow. *S. viminalis*, the Osier Willow, is grown for its branches used in the making of baskets. It grows from 10 to 20 feet.

---

57. *Salix babylonica*, weeping willow.

58. *Salix alba*, white willow.

59. Leaves of *Salix Caprea* (above left), *S. cinerea* (above right), and *S. alba*, with catkins.

Populus nigra var. *italica*, family *Saliacceae* Considered a variety of the black poplar, the term *italica* indicates its probable origin in Italy. Populus is a name given by the early Romans.

Morphology. This tree is well known for its slender, towering habit. The numerous branches from the base to the top of the trunk ascend almost vertically, as do the secondary branches, forming a compact, spindle-shaped top that moves with the wind. It can attain 100 to 130 feet.

The brown-grey bark is coarsely fissured and rough; the trunk is straight, often with basal buttressing; the twigs are slender, somewhat angular; the leaves are almost rhombic, with a wedge-shaped base and a pointed tip, toothed near the tip and smooth; the long, elastic petiole allows them to rustle in the slightest breeze.

The black poplar is a dioecious plant, but no female plants of Lombardy poplar exist. The pendulous male catkins, reddish in colour, appear in abundance before the leaves. Female plants found are probably hybrids between this tree and other poplars.

Since this tree must be propagated vegetatively, we are dealing with a clone, probably derived from a bud mutation and then propagated for its aesthetic value. There have been indications of its cultivation since the beginning of the eighteenth century in Lombardy, where it probably originated: now it is known throughout the world. It is extremely fast growing, outstripping other trees in the garden, its annual growth being from three to five feet.

Cultivation. As is generally true of all poplars, this tree likes light, loose soil in which it may broadly spread its vigorous root system. It is resistant to cold but, because of the earliness of leafing-out in spring and the retaining of foliage late in autumn, it may be damaged by late-spring and early-autumn frosts. It has no special water requirements.

The Lombardy poplar is planted in rows along the sides of roads, lanes and waterways; it is also useful as a screen or a high fence.

The list of misfortunes that can strike poplars is very long; it may be that, after fruit trees, poplars are the broadleaved trees most attacked by disease and insects.

The Lombardy poplar is no exception, and may be infested by chewing and sucking insects, and by borers. Control is difficult. It is susceptible to rust and other diseases. Several fungi attack the wood, and in damp places *Armillaria* may develop on the roots. Bacteriosis, rather dangerous on some poplars, does not infest the Lombardy. The tree is also susceptible to frost damage, and to breakage in high winds.

Other species. *P. alba*, sometimes called Abele or White Poplar is an ornamental species common in Britain, Europe and northern Asia. Its leaves are green above and white beneath. Its variety *Richardii* has leaves yellow above, white beneath.

60, 61. *Populus nigra* var. *italica*. Lombardy poplar.

32

Birch

Betula pendula, family Betulaceae

The genus is an old Latin name; the species name refers to the drooping habit of the secondary branches. The common name is Silver birch. It is a most beautiful tree; the young dark brown twigs have a purple sheen and the bottom of the trunk carries contrasting black patches.

Morphology. Silver birch has characteristics that make it unmistakable: its milk-white trunk; a bark that sheds a thin papery skin (cracked at the base only in older trees); and its sparse, thin crown, which moves in the slightest breeze. The leaves are rhomboid, pointed, doubly notched, carried on long petioles, and attached to strong, slender branches.

Varieties. Nurserymen sometimes call this tree by the Linnaean name *Betula alba*, a collective species that was later divided into *B. pendula*, *B. pubescens*, distinguished by smooth twigs and ovate, pubescent leaves, and *B. papyrifera*, the paper birch. For the same reason, it is incorrect to use *B. alba pendula* to indicate forms with particularly drooping branches. These are, instead, *B. pendula* var. *tristis*, with rather thin branches hanging straight down, and var. *gracilis*, which is similar, but with less abundant foliage.

A decorative effect is achieved by the variety *purpurea*, with dark red leaves bronze-green in autumn. The variety *dalecarlica* has pointed leaves, somewhat triangular and deeply lobed. Variety *fastigiata* has a columnar habit similar to the Lombardy poplar.

In North East America *B. nigra*, the River Birch, produces fine specimens up to 60 feet. It has a shaggy cream-coloured trunk and grows equally well away from water or near to it.

Origin. The birch is native to Europe and Asia, and is spread throughout the Alps up to 5,000 feet and in the moorlands of the high plains.

Cultivation. In the natural state it grows in full sun, forming sparse forests and avoiding mutual competition. It is a pioneer plant, occupying abandoned fields and pastures, and prefers an acid, moist, but well-drained soil. It tolerates extreme cold.

Since the tree gives little shade, it is grown for its aesthetic value, in small groups or copses, to highlight the autumnal golden yellow foliage against a background of green lawn. The low-density of its shade allows many bulbs and flowering plants to thrive beneath it.

The wood of some varieties is used for making bobbins, fish cakes and veneers. Trunks that have retained their bark are used in rustic fences, although they do not last. The bark is used in baskets. In some countries the sap is used in brewing birch beer.

The tree propagates easily by seed in a loose, mineral soil, covered lightly with earth. Many insects and diseases attack the leaves, the shoots, and the wood, but without epidemic effects.

62, 63. Group of *Betula pendula*, and detail with fruit.

62

Hornbeam

Carpinus Betulus, family Betulaceae
This genus name was given by the early Romans.

Morphology. It is a tree of modest size, usually not taller than 50 to 60 feet, with a trunk that is never round, but somewhat spirated, covered with a grey, fluted bark, even at an advanced age. The crown is dense and round. The alternate leaves are deciduous, oval, acute or pointed, with a serrated edge and numerous veins, dark green above, lighter underneath.

The tree is monoecious and flowers appear in spring together with the leaves. The males are pendant catkins, about an inch long; the females are shorter and less conspicuous, but develop a much showier fruit of trilobed leafy bracts surrounding small achene-like nuts.

Varieties. Horticultural varieties include *asplenifolia*, cut-leaved, *japonica*, of sturdy pyramidal habit, and *pendula* with long weeping branches. Native to China is *C. Turczaninovii* var. *ovalifolia*, of graceful habit and tinted young growths, that reaches 25 feet.

Cultivation. *Carpinus Betulus* is a forest tree native to Europe and western Asia, rather shade-loving, typical of mixed hardwood forests of the plains and hills having plentiful rainfall and a fertile, acid soil. It is a slow-growing plant with a short life.

This tree withstands severe pruning well and is useful to form green arches, high hedges and screens which take on a yellow colour in the autumn.

Propagation is by seed. Branches that touch the earth may root. If plants are to be used in hedges, seedlings must be transplanted at the end of the first year and well spaced in order to obtain vigorous trees. The varieties are propagated by grafting on the species.

The hornbeam is injured by early frost in autumn or in late spring; sudden and excessive changes in temperature may cause damage. *C. caroliniana*, known as American Hornbeam, is similar to *C. Betulus*.

64, 65. Male and female flowers of *Carpinus Betulus*.

66, 67. Branch with fruit and detail of leaves and fruit of *Carpinus Betulus*.

68

69

70

71

72

73

Beech

Fagus sylvatica, family Fagaceae
The generic name is taken from the Latin, while the species name recalls the forest habitat.

Morphology. The Common beech is a broad-leaved tree of an imposing habit, up to 100 feet tall. It has a smooth ash-grey bark with a hemispherical form in isolated specimens and dense foliage.

Leaves are alternate, oval or elliptical, pointed, entire or almost so, wavy at the edges, dark green and shiny on top, lighter and dull beneath, rust-coloured when dry, and sometimes persist on the tree for much of the winter.

The male flowers are pendulous heads, and the females are in pairs in an axillary involucre. They bloom in spring as the leaves appear; the seeds (beechnuts) are brown three-angled nuts. It is a gregarious tree and so is frequently found in small groups or making up much of an expansive woodland. If in competition with other species it is likely to emerge dominant because its roots take fairly rapidly to the top soil.

Varieties. Some varieties of beech are widely grown in parks. Especially noteworthy among these are: *atropunicea*, the Copper beech with dark red leaves; *laciniata*, the Cutleaf beech; *asplenifolia*; *pendula*, the Weeping beech with

74

Plane tree

Platanus acerifolia, family Platanaceae
The genus derives from its ancient Greek name. The name acerifolia refers to the resemblance of its leaves to those of the maples. The tree is frequently and incorrectly called sycamore. This species is the London plane tree.

Origin. This tree is considered by most botanists to be a hybrid between *Platanus orientalis*, of the Balkans and Asia Minor, and *P. occidentalis*, of North America, but some believe it to be a mutation of *P. orientalis*. It is the plane tree most commonly grown in Europe. In America, *P. occidentalis* is the more common. Several London squares retain the plane trees originally laid out in the eighteenth century, Berkeley Square and Lincoln's Inn Fields being good examples.

Morphology. This tree may reach 100 feet in height. It has a robust habit, a trunk often thickened at the base and covered with a particular kind of bark, scaly in the lower parts and shedding in thin plates producing vari-coloured pastel tones ranging from cream-white through greenish to light brown, leaving the trunk almost smooth. The branches are thick and form a more or less globular crown, which gives good shade. The leaves are deciduous, petioled, palmate with 3 to 5 lobes and prominent veins. They are variable in form, and intermediate between those of the two parents; the leaves are more sharply subdivided in the oriental plane tree and have very shallow lobes in the American plane tree.

The small male and female flowers (the tree is monoecious) are similar to each other, but on separate peduncles; the fruit is pendant, spherical, and persistent during winter. In spring the fruit releases the small seeds, each with long reddish hairs that facilitate dissemination.

Varieties. Two varieties with variegated leaves exist, *Suttneri*, variegated white, and *Kelseyana*, yellow. A third variety, *pyramidalis*, is of pyramidal habit. *P. occidentalis*, the Buttonwood or American plane, grows to 150 feet in southern parts of the U.S.A. but is seldom seen in Britain.

Cultivation. The plane tree succeeds best in deep, cool soil, but is rather adaptable, surviving even with asphalt up to its base; it prefers full sun, is resistant to cold, and is somewhat resistant to air pollutants. Dry soil is unsuitable.

The plane is good as a street tree and along highways. It is valued for its hardiness, its adaptability to pruning and shaping, and for the decorativeness of its foliage and bark.

The wood of the tree, rather heavy and hard, ordinarily has little value.

It is propagated by seed protected from direct sun; after two years it is transplanted. It may be propagated by cuttings taken from mature branches with a spur, in June or later, under glass, and this is the method generally recommended as the tree often does not set fertile seed. Developed specimens may be moved easily.

branches reaching to the ground; *purpurea*, the Purple beech; *tricolor* with whitish leaves dotted with green and edged with pink.

Origin. The Common Beech is native to Britain, and to Central and Southern Europe where it is found in Alpine and Appenine valleys from 2,500 to 6,000 feet up.

Cultivation. It prefers a well-drained soil of limestone origin but grows well in acid soil provided it is not overleached. The beech is suitable for large parks, assuming a quite massive size, and is also a good seaside tree. For good growth, it needs much open space around it.

The ornamental varieties are propagated by grafts on the species, ordinarily in the greenhouse in early spring; because of the heavy water requirements of the plant, grafts in the open do not ordinarily give good results. The seeds, which are difficult to keep, are sown one inch deep in March or April in rows 15 inches apart. Gun stocks, joiners' tools and the curved portions of wooden wheels are made from the timber.

---

68. Branch and fruit of *Fagus sylvatica*.

69, 70. Variously coloured leaves of *Fagus sylvatica* var. *tricolor*.

71. Incised leaves of *Fagus sylvatica* var. *asplenifolia*.

72. Prostrate shape of *Fagus sylvatica* var. *pendula*.

73. Crown of *Fagus sylvatica* var. *purpurea*.

---

74. *Platanus acerifolia* in autumn.

75. Scaly bark of *Platanus acerifolia*.

Sweet gum

Liquidambar Styraciflua, family Hamamelidaceae
The name of the genus means "liquid amber" in Latin because of the sap produced by the tree, and is recalled in the species name composed of a Greek word, "styrax", and the Latin "fluere", to secrete. The common name is Sweet Gum.

Morphology. This tree, of smaller size in cultivation, exceeds 100 feet in nature. It has a regular, dense crown, spreading if isolated, and a brown-grey trunk with bark deeply fissured longitudinally. The branches develop corky wings. Leaves are alternate, deciduous, palmate, with 5 to 7 triangular lobes somewhat star shaped and minutely serrated, shiny on top, dull and lighter underneath with a long petiole. They have the odour of balsam if crushed.

The flowers are small and devoid of petals; the males in spikes, the females in heads. The fruit is formed towards the end of summer on a long peduncle and is a dense, spherical head of compact capsules, persisting through the winter. The seeds are winged.

Varieties. There exists a choice form in California by the name Palo Alto, which develops an orange-red leaf colour in the autumn. There are also varieties *formosana*, growing from 60 to 80 feet, and *orientalis*. In Britain the trees do not attain the maximum height.

Origin. *L. Styraciflua* is native to the U.S., *L. formosana* originated in China and *L. orientalis* in Asia Minor.

Cultivation. In its natural state it is found in forests and in the damp soil along rivers that is flooded part of the year but not swampy. In cultivation it needs cool soil and full exposure to the sun; it tolerates cold to about −5°F. Growth is slow but the tree is long-lived. In Britain it rarely exceeds half of its height in the wild.

The Sweet Gum has handsome autumnal tints in its foliage, usually red-crimson, sometimes golden-yellow or orange-red.

The aromatic resin, extracted by incision of the trunk, was once used in the manufacture of chewing gum and contains compounds of cinnamic acid and an essential oil; the balm is listed in pharmocopoeia as a curative for certain diseases of the skin and is used in perfumes as a fixative. The timber is used chiefly for panelling. The sapwood and heartwood have different names commercially; the former is hazel pine, the latter satin walnut and red gum.

Propagation is by seed sown for horticultural purposes $\frac{1}{8}$ inch deep in sandy soil outdoors. The seed is stratified as soon as mature; most seed will not germinate until the second year. Cuttings of new growth roots will do well if planted in the autumn. At time of transplantation the plant should be pruned to enhance survival.

---

76. Leaf detail of *Liquidambar Styraciflua.*

77. Branch of *Liquidambar Styraciflua* with palmate leaves, here shown in early autumn.

78. *Celtis australis.*

Hackberry

Celtis australis, family Ulmaceae
The name *Celtis* was in use among the Romans centuries ago.

Morphology. This is a tall tree, often referred to as the Nettle Tree, that grows up to 70 feet, with a vigorous trunk that is grooved or somewhat warty, greyish, with strong limbs and thin branches. The crown is dense and globular, with deciduous, oval-lanceolate leaves, sharply pointed at the tip, thick, veined, dark green and rough on top, grey-green and downy beneath.

The flowers are small and inconspicuous; the stone fruits, on a peduncle, are almost spherical, about the size of peas, violet-black, with a large, wrinkled nut and a sweetish pulp, sought by the birds.

The root system is foraging and permits the tree to grow in rock clefts and among boulders and in drought areas. Growth is relatively slow but the tree is long-lived, up to 300 years and more.

Origin. *Celtis australis* is native to Southern Europe, Northern Africa, and Western Asia, and in warm areas can be found at an altitude of 3,000 feet.

Cultivation. It is essentially sun-loving, yet its hardy character makes it adaptable to rocky, dry soil. When young, it may be injured by severe freezing, but later tolerates —5°F cold.

It is used in reforestation as a preparatory species in poor soil. At one time it was cultivated for its branches, which are flexible and were used for making whip handles. The wood is tough and springy and has some use for tools and carriage making. The fruit is edible and laxative; the flowers attract bees.

This tree is sometimes employed to form shady lanes because of its hardiness and the good shade it furnishes.

Propagation is by planting mature seeds in spring; after 2 to 3 years the seedlings may be transplanted with ease. Shoots can be layered in spring or autumn. Ordinary soil is suitable. The tree likes a position in a sunny shrubbery where it should be planted from October to February.

Other species. *C. occidentalis* is the native American tree, generally with broader leaves, and orange-red to dark purple fruit. It is more resistant to cold than the European species, and grows up to 130 feet.

C. Bungeana, native to Northern China reaches 25 feet. Another species native to the southern states of America is *C. laevigata* (sometimes called *C. mississippiensis*) that grows to 60 feet and has long narrow leaves.

Magnolia

Magnolia grandiflora, family Magnoliaceae
The genus Magnolia is named after Pierre Magnol, director of the Botanic Garden at Montpelier. The species term refers to the size of the flower, which reaches diameters of 8 to 12 inches. It was first seen in Britain in 1734.

Morphology. This is an evergreen tree, with an ovoid or conical-cylindrical crown, with a smooth, grey bark, about 15 to 20 feet tall in Britain, but in the swamp lands of America has occasionally reached 100 feet. The leaves are alternate, large, narrowly elliptical to ovate, entire, thick, leathery, with a pointed tip and wedge-shaped base. They are from 3 to 4 inches

79

80

81

82

83

84

long and 1 or 2 inches wide, shiny on top, dull and lighter or rust-coloured underneath, with edges curved in towards the underside.

Flowers are white, with 6 to 12 concave, large, white petals that are fragrant; they appear from May to September according to district, May flowers being seen only in the warmest areas. The fruit is an ovate cone covered with rusty down; the seeds are in a coral-red covering, although in Britain these cones are rarely borne.

Varieties. The known varieties differ little from the species (*lanceolata, gloriosa, rotundifolia* and *gallissouiensis*).

Origin. This is the only magnolia with evergreen leaves that is widely grown; it grows naturally in the humid plains of the Gulf of Mexico and along the U.S. Atlantic coast, where it tolerates flooding if not too prolonged.

Cultivation. This plant prefers an acid, fertile, and cool soil and ample space must be provided. It is resistant to 0° or −5°F but hard frost, rapid decreases in temperature, and strong winds may cause damage to leaves and branches.

This tree is best when grown as a specimen, and is of value for its shiny foliage and for its showy and prolonged flowering.

It is propagated by seed, which must be fully ripe and stratified in moist soil or sand until spring. The resinous aril is removed before storage. It is sown in the greenhouse and transplanted to pots at the appearance of true leaves; in July it is transplanted to a larger pot, and the specimen is ready to plant in its permanent position the following year; it is best to use young plants with a ball of soil to ensure their survival. Varieties are propagated by grafting. The plant can be pruned to maintain a full, dense crown.

Other species. Many deciduous magnolias are grown for their short but spectacular spring bloom, showier than *grandiflora* because of the absence of foliage.

Magnolia denudata, from China, is a tree that may reach 30 feet, with large, bell-shaped, white flowers, and obovate leaves. *M. liliflora*, from China and Japan, is sometimes designated *M. purpurea* because of the colour of the flowers.

M. Sieboldi, from Japan and Korea, grows to 30 feet, has white, fragrant flowers in the shape of a cup which appear with the leaves.

M. Soulangeana, a hybrid between *M. denudata* and *M. liliflora*, has precocious flowers, white inside and purple outside, with obovate or obovate-oblong leaves. This species and *M. stellata* are suitable for greenhouse culture.

M. stellata is shrubby and has an extravagant white display of star-shaped flowers (rosy in one variety), before the leaves appear.

79. *Magnolia liliflora*, in bloom.

80. Corolla of *Magnolia grandiflora*.

81, 84. *Magnolia Soulangeana* and detail of the flower.

82, 83. *Magnolia stellata* in bloom and detail of the flower.

85

Tulip tree

Liriodendron Tulipifera, family Magnoliaceae
The generic name is from two Greek words, *lyrion* (lily) and *dendron* (tree) since the flowers appear something like certain species of lilies; *tulipifera* means "tulip-bearing", an attempt to establish a relationship between the two flowers. It was first introduced into Britain in the mid-seventeenth century.

Morphology. The tulip tree is majestic, growing from 100 to 135 feet high, with a cylindrical, erect trunk and grey bark deeply fissured longitudinally. It has upright limbs with the branches more or less arched downwards. The tree has an oval, sparse form.

The deciduous leaves are of a particular form —the side lobes are pointed, separated from the central third lobe by a wide gap; the latter is truncated and incised at the centre; the petiole is long, the upper surface bluish-green, somewhat shiny, the lower surface lighter and dull. In autumn they turn to gold.

The flowers, lightly fragrant, open in May and June after the leaves, and are about 2 inches in diameter, are erect, in the shape of a conch shell, consisting of 6 light yellow-green petals with orange spots on the outside. The fruit is cone shaped and contains numerous samaras, each with a lanceolate wing that becomes free in the autumn; the axil of the fruit persists on the tree.

Varieties. The following varieties are to be noted: *fastigiatum*, narrow pyramid form; *integrifolium*, with lobeless leaves; *aureomaculatum*, with gold-mottled leaves.

Origin. The tulip tree is a forest plant of alluvial, sandy, damp but well-drained soil, native to the U.S. from Massachusetts to Florida and Mississippi, where it grows alone or mixed with other broadleaves.

Cultivation. This is a sun-loving species, and needs light and space. It is resistant to cold (some specimens have resisted as low as −20°F). Growth is rapid; the tree may live for 300 years.

It is used as a specimen tree in parks, or in rows; it is remarkable when in flower and when the foliage turns to brown and gold in autumn.

The wood, light and soft, has many uses, for plywood, furniture, carpentry, and pulp. At one time the inside of the bark, bitter with the presence of liriodendrin, was used as a tonic. The tree is frequently and erroneously called "poplar".

Propagation is by seed sown in autumn or by layering in spring; varieties are grafted or propagated cuttings. Transplanting is tenuous because the fleshy roots dry rapidly in the sun and should be done in spring.

85. Tulip-tree in autumn.

86. *Liriodendron Tulipifera* with flower and leaves.

86

Tamarisk

Tamarix gallica, family Tamaricaceae
The generic name of this tree was in use among the Romans; the term *gallica* indicates the plant was first found in Gaul, now known as France. The common name is Tamarisk. It comes from the Hebrew word *tamaris* meaning a sweeping broom and the foliage is certainly broom-like.

Morphology. Tamarisk is a shrub or small tree, 10 to 30 feet high, with long, slender, weak, curved twigs. The brown or reddish-brown bark is covered with numerous plump lenticels in a series of rings; the bark fissures only at advanced age. The leaves are very small, blue-green, rhombic-ovate, sheathed, close together, half-embracing the stem, semitransparent and smooth.

Flowers appear from May to July; they are small but numerous, grouped in cylindrical racemes above and around the branches and form large panicles. There are 5 pale rose petals; the fruit is a three-sided capsule containing seeds having a tuft of hairs at the tip.

Varieties. *T. anglica*, the Common Tamarisk with white and pink flowers, is an evergreen like *T. gallica*, and is native to Britain. *T. gallica*, var. *mannifera* native to Asia Minor, provides a white honey-like secretion that is eaten by desert-dwellers in those areas.

Cultivation. Tamarisk is a typical halophyte species (literally, salt-loving) that thrives on damp shores tolerating brackish water and salt spray. It is also suited to soil that is extremely calcareous, compacted, and poorly aerated, or to beach sand where it is often used to shore up landslides and coastal dunes because of its rapid spread. While thriving on seashores, it is resistant to cold to —5°F. It is frequently used as a low windbreak.

In gardens south of the Trent it is grown as specimen near water, or in hedges, and is particularly ornamental during flowering.

The wood of tamarisk, subject to splitting and twisting, has no particular value. The bark is rich in tannin.

It may be propagated by seed, which should be barely covered with soil or, more often, by cuttings of mature or green wood. To obtain a good growth of new branches, it is necessary to prune lightly.

Other species. Rather numerous (75 to 80) and difficult to distinguish are the deciduous species of tamarisk of western Europe, the Mediterranean region, and western Asia. Among those grown as ornamentals are *Tamarix pentandra* and *T. parviflora*, the latter often confused with *T. africana*. *T. parviflora* flowers earlier, in May. *T. pentandra* flowers late.

T. hispida, a rather tender species native to the Caspian area, has pink flowers and glaucous foliage.

Fungi that attack the tamarisk cause disease of the leaves and root rot or stem rot.

87. The abundant flowering of a tamarisk.

88. *Tamarix pentandra.*

87

88

Flowering plums, cherries, almonds

Genus *Prunus*, family Rosaceae
Prunus is the Latin name for this genus. Here we describe some of its ornamental species.

Different species. *Prunus serrulata* (flowering cherry) is one of the most beautiful flowering trees we can grow, singly or in rows. It is native to China, Korea, and Japan and has numerous varieties, some with double flowers. These are almost all of Japanese origin. It is generally grown as a standard, making a tree from 15 to 30 feet. The chestnut-coloured bark flakes in concentric circles like the fruiting trees, and its bearing is similar. The leaves are oval, ovate, or obovate, pointed, smooth, somewhat blue-green and glaucous underneath, and toothed. The flowers have no fragrance, are white or rose in great profusion in early spring at leafing or just before, and are grouped in clusters of five to seven.

It is propagated by budding on *P. cerasifera* var. *atropurpurea*, the purple-leaved plum. This tree is not normally pruned. It has no particular soil requirements, and its hardiness depends on the variety. Its common name is Kwanzan. Another variety, *P. serrulata erecta* or Amana-gowa, is excellent for terraces where space is limited. From a low root stock it establishes itself as a slender upright column of one or more slim stems bearing semi-double pink blossoms.

89

90

91

92

93

Prunus japonica is a dwarf, flowering cherry, a shrubby type up to 4 feet in height, and in the variety *flore pleno* grown for its magnificent, rosy, double flowers which precede the leaves and densely cover the branches. The fruit is wine-red. This dwarf variety is a good garden plant and is commercially grown on a large scale.

P. triloba, also known as flowering almond, is a fine shrub indigenous to China. It responds best if treated as a climber. *P. triloba* var. *plena* is suitable for forcing in the greenhouse, is double flowered, and does not produce fruit.

Fruit is also rather rare in the single-flowering forms. The species name comes from the leaf shape, divided into three at the tip, widely ovate or obovate, sharply pointed, deeply and doubly serrated. The flowers are solitary on a short pedicel, are bright pink, and appear in spring with the foliage. It likes lime in the soil, and is propagated by grafting on plums which produces short-lived plants; propagation by division or root grafting on the plum is considered best. The variety *Petzoldii* does not have tri-lobed leaves.

For spots of colour and low hedges, *P. cerasifera* var. *atropurpurea* is also used. This shrub has purple-red leaves and blooms after the leaves appear in spring. It has small rosy flowers, barely visible. The fruit is spherical and red with an edible sweet-sour pulp. This tree is also resistant to cold. The typical flowering *Prunus* trees have green leaves; the purple-leaved plum is used as a rootstock for flowering cherries, as are *P. Cerasus* (sour cherry) and *P. avium* (sweet cherry).

---

89. *Prunus serrulata* (Japanese flowering cherry).

90. *Prunus triloba*.

91. *Prunus subhirtella* var. *pendula* (Rosebud cherry).

92. *Prunus cerasifera* cultivar Highan (Cherry or Myrobalan plum).

93. *Malus floribunda* (showy Crab Apple).

Mimosa and acacia

Albizzia = Acacia Julibrissin, family Leguminosae

Morphology. The mimosa is a small tree, 25 to 35 feet tall, with the spreading habit of the acacias, branches somewhat horizontal, forming a flat top. The branches are sparse and create a silky appearance because of the finely subdivided bipinnate leaves. Each leaf has 9 to 12 pairs of pinnae.

The flowers appear during July and August and are groups of heads in terminal clusters. They have no petals and are comprised of many long, diverging stamens, of a rosy colour. The trunk and limbs are devoid of spines.

Origin. This species, native to dry areas from Iran to Japan, needs full light and well-drained soil; it will not tolerate severe cold, and is not hardy in the open through the British winter.

Cultivation. The albizzia is used best as a specimen, and is very popular because of the airiness of the foliage and the showy bloom. It is sensitive to cold, is ravaged by web-worm, and is susceptible to the soil-borne verticillium wilt, which usually causes death.

Other species. Closely related to this tree are the acacias (genus *Acacia*), which are grown for cut flowers and for ornament in Mediterranean gardens and to create shady lanes. This genus is native to the dry regions of Australia, Africa and Asia, where it forms arboreal savannahs and sparse forests. In Britain it is usually treated as a greenhouse flowering shrub or small tree.

Many of the cultivated kinds vary in being either evergreen or deciduous, having either bipinnate leaves or leaves reduced to leaf-like petioles, being either tall trees or low shrubs, and being either spineless or free of spines. All, however, have small flowers that appear in late winter or early spring, with reduced petals while the long stamens form heads in large clusters, resembling golden-yellow or white wads of cotton.

Most species are grown for the flowers; others, high in tannin and having a rapid growth rate, are used in warm countries as vegetation for sand dunes to arrest shifting sand and to serve as windbreak in frost free areas. All the mimosas prefer full sun.

Propagation is by seed, but the seed-bed temperature must be kept above 60°F. Germination can be hastened by treating the seed with boiling water before sowing. If the seeds are old, this is done more than once.

Transplanting is difficult because of the long tap root; it is therefore preferable to sow in containers and transplant the seedling while very young. The ornamental types are propagated by approach grafting on *Acacia retinodes* in summer. After flowering, which occurs at the end of winter, they should be pruned to encourage thick crowns and prevent fruiting, which is not ornamental.

Acacias are also injured by hard freezing and will not tolerate temperatures below 20°F.

Various insects may damage acacias in their native habitat and where it has been cultivated for centuries, as in South Africa, for example, where it is grown for the production of tannin.

The species most grown for ornament are *A. decurrens*; *A. longifolia*; *A. Farnesiana*, used for the making of perfume; *A. podalyriaefolia*; *A. cultriformis*; *A. spectabilis*; *A. Baileyana*.

94. *Albizzia julibrissin.*

95. Close-up of *Albizzia julibrissin.*

96. Inflorescence of an acacia.

97. *Acacia Farnesiana.*

98

Redbud or judas tree

Cercis Siliquastrum, family Cesalpiniaceae
The common name derives from the legend that Judas hanged himself on this tree after betraying Christ.

Morphology. This is a deciduous tree or shrub, growing from 15 to 40 feet, with a trunk often twisted and branching down to the ground, covered with a blackish bark, extremely rough because of transverse and longitudinal cracking. The crown is broad and leggy; the leaves, round, heart-shaped, smooth, dark green on the upper surface, lighter below, on a long petiole.

Redbud flowers early in spring. The butterfly-shaped flowers are rose-lilac, and appear on the trunk, limbs and branches in thick clusters, in vivid contrast to the dark limbs and to the sprouting leaves. The fruit is a compressed pod, reddish and persistent. This tree is generally considered to be the best garden species.

Varieties. Variety *alba* has white flowers.

Origin. *C. Siliquastrum* is native to southern Europe and western Asia where it grows to an altitude of 3,000 feet. It was first introduced into Britain in the late sixteenth century.

Cercis canadensis, the American Redbud, is native to the United States from Connecticut and Pennsylvania to Michigan, west to Missouri, south to Texas and Florida. It grows to between 15 and 40 feet, and is similar in appearance and growth to *C. Siliquastrum.* The Chinese Redbud, *C. chinensis,* is potentially a small tree but in most landscape plantings is grown as a shrub.

Cultivation. *C. Siliquastrum* has a rather slow growth. It adapts well to most soil types. In the north of England grow it against a south wall.

Redbud is suited for street plantings and is grown for its attractive flowers and leaves and for its resistance to air pollutants. It may be forced in the greenhouse for cut flowers. Its wood is used for small pieces and inlay work. The flowers may be eaten in salads.

Propagation is by seed; cuttings may also be taken during September and October. Redbud is attacked by some diseases: a canker, some leaf-spots, a root rot, and two sapwood rots.

---

98. *Cercis Siliquastrum* in bloom.

99

100

Japanese pagoda tree

Sophora japonica, family Leguminosae
The name of the genus seems to be derived from the Arabic name, *sophero*, for a tree with pea-shaped flowers; the name of the species shows that the tree originated in Japan. It was introduced into Britain in the middle of the eighteenth century.

Morphology. In the type species this is a tree of rather lofty stature (65 to 80 feet), with a broad rounded crown, not very dense, with a straight cylindrical trunk having a grey bark slightly fissured longitudinally.

The limbs are broad and twisted; the branches are slender, shiny, and are green. The deciduous leaves are unequally pinnate, with 7 to 17 oval-acute, entire, smooth, dark green leaflets, shiny on top and blue-green underneath.

It blooms in August and September, depending on temperature, in large, loose, terminal panicles, with yellowish white butterfly-like flowers having a pleasing aroma. The pod, about an inch long, resembles a string of beads.

Varieties. Among the varieties, there is *violacea* whose flower has both purplish wings and keel and whose leaves are densely hairy underneath.

S. japonica var. *pendula* is a smaller tree, growing to about 30 feet, and because of its weeping habit it must be grafted high (at least 6 feet) on a trunk of the type species. The limbs are extremely twisted in rather bizarre forms, while the thin branches are pendent but not very broad; in all, with time, a rather picturesque crown will form, which is assisted by judicious and not excessive pruning.

Cultivation. *Sophora* is adapted to most soils, provided they are deep and well drained. It needs a warm position in full sun and wall protection except in the Cornish riviera. Despite the name, in Japan the species grows only under cultivation; it is native to China and Korea.

The typical Japanese pagoda tree does not give much shade, but for its hardiness and the interesting foliage it is useful in groves and lanes. The variety *pendula* is good as a specimen tree, and the variety *variegata* has leaves margined with creamy white. Almost all parts of the plant are purgative. The flowers are visited by bees.

The typical species is propagated by seed sown in spring; the varieties by grafting on the type. *Sophora* is rarely attacked by insects; among diseases there is a wilt of the stem shoots and a root rot. Excessive pruning is harmful.

Other species. Plants of another family with a habit similar to that of the variety *pendula* (but with branches less twisted) include European Ash (*Fraxinus excelsior* var. *pendula*) and white mulberry (*Morus alba* var. *pendula*).

---

99. The typical crown of *Sophora japonica* var. *pendula*.

100. The mulberry (*Morus alba*) often has a decorative effect.

Sycamore maple

Acer Pseudo-Platanus, family Aceraceae
The name *Acer* was in use among the early Romans; the species name refers to the slight resemblance of the leaves to the plane tree.

Morphology. This tree is majestic and will attain 100 feet. It has a large, straight trunk and a dense, rather rounded top especially in isolated specimens. The bark on young trees is smooth and grey; later, scales develop that drop off gradually.

The leaves are deciduous, opposite, on a rather long petiole, large, palmate with five broadly wedge-shaped lobes deeply divided with unequally toothed edges green and shiny on top, blue-green and dull underneath, where the veining stands out in sharp relief.

The small greenish flowers, in drooping panicles, appear in April or May. The double samaras are showy, have two oval seeds, each attached to a membranous, oblong, arching wing. The two wings compose a right angle and facilitate dissemination; the wind gives them a spiral motion and carries them some distance.

Varieties. Among the varieties, those with coloured leaves are of some interest: *erythrocarpum* has shiny leaves and red fruits; *purpureum* has leaves that are purple underneath; *Worleei* has yellow leaves and a red petiole; *variegatum* has variegated leaves dotted with white; and others. *Leopoldii* is suitable for small gardens as it is slow-growing and *Handjeryi* is extremely slow-growing.

101

103

102

104

105

Origin. Sycamore maple is a rare tree occurring mixed with other broadleaves up to an altitude of 5,000 feet in the wild.

Cultivation. It thrives on various soils if not too compact. It prefers full sun, although it tolerates shade when young. In culture it does not have particular requirements. It grows rapidly and will live from 500 to 700 years.

It is used for shady lanes because of its vigour and the shade given by the top, while isolated specimens create an interesting effect, especially in autumn when the leaves acquire a warm golden-yellow colour.

Propagation is by seed; the varieties are grafted in summer. Leaves are disfigured by spots caused by a fungus, *Rhytisma acerinum*.

Other species. *Acer platanoides* (Norway maple) recognizable by the rather acute tips of its leaf lobes, grows up to 50 feet in height.

The box elder (*A. Negundo*) is widely grown for its wide adaptation. Forms with variegated leaves are of particular interest. It may be used in small plantings, tolerates pruning, but is subject to wind breakage.

---

101. Flowering branches of *Acer Pseudo-Platanus*.

102, 104. *Acer Negundo* with variegated leaves, and a flowering branch.

103. *Acer platanoides* cultivar "Fassen's black".

105. Detail of the foliage of *Sophora japonica* var. *pendula*.

106

107

108

109

110

111

Japanese maple

Acer palmatum, family Aceraceae
The species name refers to the leaf shapes which appear in numerous forms. The tree has spread throughout the world because of the aesthetic value of the various cultivars that originated in Japan and Korea, each distinguished by a local name.

Morphology. This is a shrub or small tree, 25 feet or less, that acquires a picturesque and "Japanese" look with its thick, twisted trunk, branching from the base. The trunk is smooth and greyish and the crown is dense and spreading. The leaves are small and smooth, palmate, with 5 to 9 sharp lobes, in varied forms and colours among the varieties. Varieties vary in form: fully-leaved limbs to those with leaves on only a third of the limb; lobes vary from linear to broad; edges may be incised, toothed, or almost entire. As to colour, leaves may be of a single shade or of varied colours: green, red, completely purple, or any of these, with edges in carmine, yellow, green with white spots, green with a rosy border, yellow green with dark green borders and veins, spotted with white, pink, or red, etc.; the different forms and colours of the leaves combine variously together. The colours, furthermore, vary considerably during the year, with delicate pastel tints in spring when the leaves develop, while in autumn the colours become more intense; even the green types acquire rosy or red, yellow or orange shades in autumn.

The flowers, small and purplish, are in erect

112

113

114

115

Horse chestnut or buckeye

corymbs; the fruits, as in other maples, are double-winged in an obtuse angle.

Cultivation. The soil should be fertile, slightly acid, and well drained. It is a slow-growing species of great horticultural interest, valued for the elegant, light foliage and the various colourations it may acquire. Because of its small size, it lends itself well in warm areas to gardens on terraces and balconies, grown in tubs. Otherwise it should be potted in a cool greenhouse.

The varieties are propagated by grafting in March, by layering in October, or by budding for the choice Japanese kinds in August. Seeds can be sown $\frac{1}{4}$ inch deep in October.

Other species. Another maple of the same origin, *Acer japonicum*, is often grown under the same common name. It is distinguished by leaves with 9 to 11 small lobes and deeply-toothed edges.

---

106. *Acer palmatum*, with purple leaves.

107. *Acer japonicum*.

108. Bronze form of *Acer palmatum* with heavily subdivided leaves.

109. *Acer palmatum* in spring.

110. Foliage of *Acer palmatum*.

111. *Acer palmatum*, cultivar "Koko".

Aesculus Hippocastanum, family Hippocasta-naceae

In classical Latin the name *aesculus* indicated a kind of oak; the fruit of this tree, resembling chestnuts, was believed to cure diseases of the horse. It was described in 1557 by Mattioli and around the beginning of the seventeenth century was widely used at Versailles; it was extensively planted by Cardinal Richelieu and used a great deal by Le Notre in his gardens *a la francaise*.

Morphology. This tree, reaching 100 feet, is characterized by its robust trunk covered with scaly grey-brown bark, and for the compact crown, and thick, almost erect, limbs. The leaves are opposite, digitate-palmate, with 5 to 7 sessile leaflets, wedge-shaped at the base and rounded to a point at the tip, and doubly toothed.

The flowers are very showy, composed of 5 wavy, white petals, spotted with red, in erect terminal panicles. The fruits are large, spherical, and spiny, and contain 1 to 3 large, round, or hemispherical, shiny reddish-brown seeds with a pale hilar scar.

Varieties. Varieties include *luteovariegata*, *variegata*, *incisa*, *laciniata*, *pyramidalis*; the variety *Baumannii* has double, sterile, white flowers. An interesting form is *A. carnea*, a hybrid of *A. Hippocastanum* and *A. Pavia*, which combines the height of the female parent with the red flower colour of the male. *A. turbinata* is the creamy Japanese Horse Chestnut.

Cultivation. This is a tree that readily propagates by seed. It will tolerate temperatures as low as 15 to 20 degrees below zero. Although not particularly associated with any one type of soil, it prospers in cool, fertile soil and does not grow well in damp or dry or compacted soil.

The tree is commonly used as an ornamental, either isolated or in groups, especially to make shady lanes where it is appreciated for its early leafing, the beautiful spring bloom, and its dense shade; it is not often planted as a forest tree. The wood is used for fencing, packing cases and carving. The fruit, rather rich in starch, is bitter because of its saponin content which produces a lather and thus may be used as a detergent.

Horse chestnut seed may be planted in spring after winter stratifications; in one or two years seedlings are transplanted. Varieties are grafted in March or budded in July.

It is subject to very little insect damage, but older specimens are hollowed out by wood rotting fungi; disease spots may appear on the leaves. Pollution can cause early loss of leaves.

Other species. The hybrid of the American *A. Pavia* (with thornless fruit) and the common horse chestnut is preferred as it is more rugged and capable of attaining a greater size.

112, 114 *Aesculus Hippocastanum* and inflorescence.

113, 115. *Aesculus carnea* and inflorescence.

Silver linden

Tilia tomentosa = T. argentea, family Tiliaceae *Tilia* is the classical Latin name; both species' names refer to the appearance of the underside of the leaves, which, being covered with dense down, seem silvery white.

Morphology. This is a tree some 75 to 100 feet tall with a sturdy structure, a dense, rounded oval crown, a dark grey bark with only sparse, shallow fissures. The limbs are numerous and erect, the branches spreading, the new twigs downy. The deciduous leaves are alternate, large, characteristically heart-shaped, slightly pointed, serrated, and thick with many veins.

The inflorescence, as in other lindens, consists

116

of drooping clusters with few flowers on each, carried on an adnate peduncle with an obtuse, oblong, membraneous wing, which, aided by the wind, enhances, dissemination of the fruit. The flowers have five yellow petals, are very fragrant with a sweet perfume, and appear in July. The fruit is small, ovoid, hairy, woody, and ribbed.

Varieties. *T. tomentosa* var. *pendula* is a weeping form of silver linden and is sometimes confused with *T. petiolaris*.

Origin. The silver linden is native to southeastern Europe and western Asia.

Cultivation. It is the most hardy of the genus, and has no preference as to soil; it tolerates drought better than any other species of linden. Growth is relatively rapid.

The linden is considered ornamental because of the contrast of colours of the two sides of the leaves, especially visible in a breeze. It is often used for groves and lanes and specimen trees. The strong aroma of the flowers may be annoying to some. It is not, like other lindens, honey-producing; indeed, the nectar of *T. tomentosa* and *T. petiolaris* may be toxic to bees.

Extracts of the flowers are used in medicine. The wood is valuable for inlay work, toys, and musical instruments.

Propagation is by seed gathered in autumn and stratified in cool sand until spring, when it is sown. Varieties are propagated by grafting in spring or budding in summer; the resulting specimens may have a single-stemmed crown for some years. It is also propagated by cuttings and by layering. Sprouts often develop from the roots, and these may be cut off. Transplanting is easy even for large trees.

Other species. *T. petiolaris* (Weeping White Linden) is a weeping form similar to *T. tomentosa* var. *pendula*; *T. platyphyllos* (Large-Leaved Linden) has large leaves that are velvety underneath; *T. Cordata* (Small-Leaved Linden) has small blue-green leaves, smooth on the underside but tufted with reddish hairs at the intersections of the veins; *T. europaea* is the hybrid of *T. platyphyllos* and *T. cordate* is more demanding in regard to moisture. *T. americana* (American Linden or Basswood) is also suited for lane planting. It has large thick leaves, light green underneath and smooth except for a hairiness like that on *T. Cordata. T. mongolica*, the Mongolian Linden, is a graceful species.

The foliage of lindens falls early in the autumn; it is attractive to aphids which cover the leaves with honeydew, after which a fungus with surface spores may develop disfiguring the leaves with blackish spots.

---

116. *Tilia europaea.*

117. *Tilia cordata* in bloom.

118. Winged fruit of a linden.

119. *Tilia tomentosa.*

120, 121. Flowering panicle and leaves with fruit of *Paulownia tomentosa.*

122, 123. *Catalpa bignonioides* and details of flowers.

117

119

118

120

121

122

Paulownia

Paulownia tomentosa, family Scrophulariceae. ariceae.

Morphology. This is a medium-sized tree, rarely as tall as 50 feet, but having a trunk of large diameter, with a grey bark. The crown is formed of thick, crooked limbs and branches and is spreading, sometimes umbrella-shaped. The deciduous leaves are opposite, large (the outer ones very large), on a long petiole, oval to heart-shaped, entire or with obtuse lobes at the sides, hairy and greyish beneath, smooth on top.

The flowers are rather showy and are initiated in the autumn preceding bloom; they open in early spring before the leaves. They are carried in erect panicles and are large, tubular, pale lilac-violet, with darker spots inside, opening at the tip in five unequal lobes arranged with two lips, in form foxglove-shaped.

The fruits are a large, rather woody, inverted pear-shaped capsule, persisting and conspicuous over winter. After being cut down, the tree re-grows with great vigour from the stump, producing shoots up to 6 feet at the end of the first year, with leaves more than 20 inches long.

Varieties. Variety *lanata* has a yellow down on the underside of the leaves; variety *pallida* has pale flowers.

Origin. This tree is native to China and was introduced into Britain in the nineteenth century.

Cultivation. It prefers a deep, fertile, moist soil; it grows poorly in calcareous or dry soil. Because it continues growth unusually late in the year, the shoots that are not yet mature may be damaged by frost, and the following year's bloom may be spoiled. Woody branches can tolerate temperature as low as −5°F. It grows rapidly.

This is a fine ornamental tree, suited as a specimen and for planting in city squares and lanes because of its small size, its beautiful flowers, and the shade it affords, even though the foliage is not especially elegant.

It is propagated by seed in spring or by root-cuttings, or greenwood cuttings, sown $\frac{1}{8}$ inch deep in sandy loam in a cold frame.

Other species. *P. lilacina* is a species growing to about 50 feet. In the closely related Bignoniaceae family is a similar tree, *Catalpa bignonioides* native to the southeastern United States, which may at first sight be confused with paulownia when it is in leaf, the leaves being more or less of the same form and size in both species. Close observation, however, shows that the leaves are opposite in paulownia and in whorls of three in catalpa. The catalpa flowers are white, with yellow or red markings inside, having a broader edge and shorter tubule; the fruit is an elongated pod, 8 to 15 inches long, resembling a bean. It is also ornamental. It prefers light soil and is more hardy than paulownia. In height it ranges from 25 to 50 feet, and has an attractive variety, *aurea*.

Flowering shrubs

Chimonanthus

Chimonanthus praecox = Calycanthus praecox, family Calycanthaceae

The generic name means "winter flower", from the Greek *keimon* and *anthos*; the other generic name comes from the Latin meaning chalice because of the development of the calyx; species name refers to the earliness of flowering. It was introduced into Britain in the middle of the eighteenth century.

Morphology. This shrub grows to about 10 feet, has many stems with arching principal branches and erect secondary growth. The bark is a light grey-brown, sprinkled with numerous large lenticels like warts. The leaves are opposite, entire, oval or oblong, about 6 inches long, shiny on top, and almost sessile.

The flowers, on short, scaly twigs from the growth of the previous year, appear from December to March, depending on the temperature; they are single or in pairs, with several petal-like sepals, oval or elongated, waxy yellow and longer at the outside, veined and suffused with purple at the inside. There are 5 or 6 short stamens and many pistils. The fruit is capsule-shaped with many achene-like seeds.

Varieties. Among the varieties are *grandiflora*, with larger flowers; *concolor*, with entirely yellow flowers; *parviflorus*, with small flowers.

There is also a variety with purple flowers.

Cultivation. *Chimonanthus* is a native of China and it must be planted in a warm, sheltered position to obtain bloom in winter. It has no particular soil requirements. It is a shrub to be recommended because, in temperate climates, it is one of the very few to bloom in winter. The corollas are fragrant, with a sweet and penetrating odour that is used in making perfumes.

Propagation is by seed sown in spring, or by cuttings taken in summer, or by layering in September or October.

Other species. Another winter-flowering shrub, not widely grown, is *Hamamelis mollis*. This is an early blooming Witch Hazel that reaches a height of 10 feet, producing flowers even at low temperatures which are not damaged even if the thermometer goes below the freezing point. The bare branches are covered with aromatic flowers having four linear, twisted, golden yellow petals, and a short cup-shaped purple-red calyx. The leaves resemble hazelnut and are vividly coloured in autumn. It is propagated by seed or by layering in October or November. Grafting can be done using the stock of *H. virginiana*.

124. *Chimonanthus fragrans.*

125. *Hamamelis mollis.*

124

125

126

127

128

129

Hydrangeas

Genus *Hydrangea*, family Saxifragaceae
The name of the genus is from the Greek *hydor* meaning water, and *aggeion* meaning vase, referring thus to the cup-shaped fruit.

Morphology. There follows a complete description of the most widespread type, *Hydrangea macrophylla*, which, according to Rehder, includes 22 principal varieties (among which is the garden hydrangea) and numerous horticultural forms and cultivars. *H. Hortensia* and *H. opuloides* are older names for *H. macrophylla*.

The general characteristics of this decorative pot species are: a shrubby bush (woody at the base), as tall as 12 feet, with smooth stems; large ovate to ovate-elliptical leaves, pointed or acute, serrated; inflorescence in broad, umbrella-shaped cymes, composed partially or entirely of sterile flowers that have a broad calyx with four large sepals, more or less oval, with a variable edge and vivid colour (the fertile flowers are small and much less conspicuous).

The flowers range from white through pink to violet, depending somewhat on the soil pH (the acidity-alkalinity balance) and the aluminium content of the soil. In calcareous soil, the varieties with violet flowers do not have this colour at all, but are pink. The flowers appear in June and July; the fruit is a capsule.

Origin. *H. macrophylla* is native to Japan and China. Many varieties have been introduced from these countries, the first coming to Britain in the early eighteenth century.

Cultivation. The plant will not tolerate temperatures below 15°F, so that in northern areas the tops freeze back in some winters. It prefers a fertile, well-drained, cool soil and tolerates shade but grows and flowers best in full sun with adequate moisture.

It is suited for borders, groups, foundation plantings and hedges. Types with large flowering heads composed of sterile flowers and large, broad, vividly-coloured sepals are grown in pots and forced to flower in winter in the greenhouse. They are vigorous and may be used as flowering potted plants.

Hydrangeas are easily propagated by division or by softwood cuttings under glass in summer. To get large flowering heads, it is necessary to prune rather severely each autumn or, in cold regions, at the beginning of spring.

Many troubles afflict hydrangeas including various diseases and insects and a nematode.

Other species. Among related species, the panicled hydrangea, *H. paniculata*, is very ornamental; this has small flowers, all sterile or almost so, white (tending with time to purple), borne in a compact, elongated florescence. It grows to 30 feet and has thin, woody branches. It also is grown in tubs and has requirements similar to those of the formerly mentioned species. It is native to China and Japan. *H. paniculata* var. *grandiflora* (Peegee Hydrangea) is the common outdoor hydrangea.

H. petiolaris is little known. It is native to Japan, has many branches, a vine climbing to 50 feet, and roots easily; it has white flowers of mixed types.

H. Sargentiana, native to China, has pale violet flowers, large velvety leaves and grows to 6 feet. Mildew is common on hydrangeas in Britain, especially among those grown under glass. Brown spots with a marked red border on the leaves is occasionally found on *H. Hortensia*. On hydrangeas sold by florists ringspot sometimes causes lesions and distortions of the leaves. Most varieties are resistant enough to tolerate the disease without suffering severe damage, although there is the possibility that some individual plants will thereby be rendered unsaleable. For the outdoor culture of *H. Sargentiana* the shrub should be planted October to November or March to April. Dead and straggling shoots need to be pruned in March and a top-dressing given annually. Young growth of this variety will be injured by early spring frosts and so needs protection. *H. paniculata* and *H. arborescens* need annual pruning to within one inch of the base, and free watering is called for in dry weather. *H. xanthoneura*, also from China, has white flowers in convex corymbs and grows to 15 feet.

126-129. The rich bloom of *Hydrangea macrophylla* in various colours.

130

131

132

Roses

Genus *Rosa*, family Rosaceae

Everybody is familiar with roses and their large number of forms and cultivars, continually increased by hybridization and selection by skilled floriculturists. Everyone is aware, also, of the various uses that this genus has in gardens, and it may well be said that the rose is queen of the flowering shrubs because of the large beautifully shaped flowers and range of colours.

Morphology. Roses are shrubs with erect or climbing habits, spiny, mostly with deciduous leaves; the leaves are alternate, almost always unequally pinnate, with large stipules; the flowers are borne singly or in clusters, are in diverse colours, often fragrant, composed of five petals in the natural state, becoming very numerous in doubled-types with the sexual organs also transformed into petals, and are characterized by pistils; the fruit is a red hip, fleshy when ripe.

The Greeks and Romans grew roses; indeed, the latter achieved winter flowering by forcing. The first catalogue of roses (describing 16

varieties) was published in Britain in 1597. Until the late eighteenth century only summer-flowering roses were known, while the ever-blooming types were obtained only about 1800 with the introduction of some Chinese varieties. An interesting illustrated monograph of old varieties, attractive also from an aesthetic point of view, is *Les Roses*, by P. J. Redoute (1817–1824), which was drawn up at the insistence of Josephine Beauharnais, wife of Napoleon I. It depicts from nature the collections of roses in the castle of Malmaison. The known varieties at that time numbered about 250.

According to Harvey, roses may be classified in the following way: hybrid teas, with large, individual flowers having several petals of varied colour, often fragrant, recurrently blooming, that are undoubtedly the most popular types of rose bush for the home gardener; floribundas (formerly called polyanthus), with semi-double or double flowers in clusters, hardy, floriferous, and long-lasting, among the most grown types; dwarf polyanthus, with a compact inflorescence and smaller flowers, suitable for edging; grandi-

133

134

135

floras, similar to floribundas but taller and with singly borne and clustered flowers on the same plant; shrub roses, comprising such ancient forms as musk roses, centifolias, damask roses, etc., now little grown; climbing, derived from *Rosa Wichuraiana* and including kinds ascribable to hybrids of tea or floribunda roses; miniature roses, of small stature; tea roses, of warm, dry climates, not now often grown, single-flowered, with their own particular aroma.

Cultivation. Sites suited to the growing of roses are exposed to full sun or are only lightly shaded (floribundas are a little less exacting in regard to light). The soil may be variable but must always be well fertilized, and well drained. Planting is done in autumn or early spring. Often, to avoid moisture loss and to control weeds, the beds are mulched. Any suckers from the root-stock should be removed. In general, pruning is severe, just above a dormant leaf bud facing outwards, with a slanting cut, preferably before growth begins in spring. Stems injured by frost or disease and dead stems are removed, and flowering stems reduced to two leaf buds. With tree roses, care should be taken not to destroy the symmetry of the crown.

Other than for flowering beds and borders and for covering walls, arches, pergolas, and pillars in the open air, roses are grown for cut flowers. The latter bloom in the greenhouse out of season and the desired form is a single flower on a long stem, which is obtained by using hybrid tea varieties with a solitary flower, removing side buds if necessary.

In the garden the hybrid teas bloom in June-July and again in September, so a continuous succession of flowers can be obtained. Indeed, in some districts blooms can be had in December.

The propagation of roses is usually by budding on a hardy type. Older varieties and climbers may be propagated by cuttings.

Many troubles beset roses. Aphids attack the underside of the leaves, the new shoots, and the flower peduncle, causing the plant to weaken, and the leaves and flower buds to be misshapen. Thrips cause spotting of the leaves and deformation of the flower buds. These insects may be controlled with appropriate insecticides. The red mite, more dangerous in the greenhouse, makes leaves turn yellow and fall.

Among diseases, the most serious are powdery mildew and black spot, which may be kept in check by frequent fungicidal sprays.

Chlorosis of the leaves in calcareous soil is due to iron deficiency and may be corrected by spraying with chelated iron or with ferrous sulphate. In spite of these drawbacks, British gardeners produce roses of outstanding beauty.

136

137

138

130-135. The cultivars of roses are so numerous as to make cataloguing them difficult. Pictured here:

130 Nymph, a polyanthus rose.

131. Blaze.

132. Romantic.

133. Baccarat, a climber.

134. Bettina

135. Gail Borden.

136. *Wisteria floribunda* with violet flowers.

Wisteria

Wisteria floribunda, family Leguminosae
The genus is dedicated to Caspar Wistar, anatomist.

Morphology. This plant is a woody vine with deciduous, unequally pinnate leaves with oval-lanceolate leaflets, silky underneath when young. The stem is twisted into spirals and can reach considerable length; it has a brown-grey bark dotted with numerous lenticels, later slightly fissured. The branches are abundant and wrap themselves around any support, including the trunk.

The flowers are quite showy, butterfly-like, of a light violet blue, fragrant, and appear in spring in drooping, terminal racemes; sometimes they have a light flowering towards the end of summer. The pods are compressed, silky, and many-seeded.

Varieties. *Alba*, *rosea*, *variegata*, *macrobotrys*, and *violaceo-plena* with double flowers, are among the best known varieties.

Origin. This species is native to Japan. It tolerates cold, requires sun, is suited to any soil, and grows to 30 feet.

Cultivation. This is the most-used climber for covering trellises, walls, and pergolas, sometimes supporting them. It is a honey plant.

The varieties and cultivars are grafted on *Wisteria frutescens*, sometimes by root graft; it also is propagated by layering, stem cuttings, root cuttings and by seed. Another species, less widespread, is *W. sinensis*, native to China, with a smaller number of leaflets in the compound leaf and with scentless flowers.

Other species. Among climbing plants *Campsis radicans*, called trumpet vine, is popular for its large, tubular flowers, opening abruptly in five rounded, irregular lobes, orange outside, red inside. The climbing stems need no assistance since they have aerial rootlets. It is a hardy, sun-loving species, preferring cool soil, and is native to the U.S. It is propagated by cuttings or layering.

137. *Wisteria floribunda* var. alba.

138, 139. *Campis radicans* and detail of the corolla.

139

140

141

Golden-chain tree and broom

Genera *Laburnum* and *Cytisus*, family Leguminosae

This group of related genera has included in the past a number of classifications which are now grouped in the two genera. They were first introduced into Britain in the late sixteenth century.

The most interesting species is *Laburnum anagyroides* (= *Cytisus Laburnum*).

Morphology. This is a small tree 20 to 30 feet tall or, in cultivated forms, an erect, branching shrub. The branches are erect or spreading, pendulous at the tips; the bark is smooth; the leaves are large, trifoliate, dark green and smooth on top, lighter and hairy underneath.

The spring flowers, fragrant, in the characteristic pea-shape, are in long, terminal, pendulous racemes, a beautiful golden yellow with a purple spot on the standard; the fruit is a pod.

Cultivation. Golden-chain tree prefers a cool, well-drained soil, and full sun. It does well in shrubberies and can be trained over arches and pergolas. To ensure regular flowering it is advisable to remove seed pods after flowering; this also keeps the tree vigorous.

The wood is hard and close-grained, and is used for small articles. All parts of the plant (leaves, flowers, and especially the fruits) are poisonous.

Propagation is by seed in March or April, or by layering; varieties are usually grafted on the type species.

Other species. *Cytisus purpureus* is distinguished from other species by its purple-white or pink flowers. It is a small plant, to about 2 feet, native to the eastern Alps. It is sometimes grafted high on the *Laburnum* to give a specimen with a developed trunk.

Common broom (*Cytisus scoparius*) is a thickly branched shrub, with thin, green branches, almost devoid of leaves, with rather large golden flowers. It is adapted to most well-drained soils, and prefers full sun. It has many varieties, differing in flower colour. It is native to Europe and particularly Britain. Other countries refer to it as Scotch broom.

---

140. *Laburnum anagyroides* (Golden-Chain Tree).

141. *Cytisus sessilifolius.*

142. *Cytisus scoparius* (Scotch Broom).

Azaleas and rhododendrons

Genus *Rhododendron*, family Ericaceae
The rhododendrons constitute a group of ornamental plants of great importance. Azaleas and rhododendrons cannot be separated botanically, although many azaleas are deciduous. The hardy varieties of rhododendrons were introduced to Britain in the mid-eighteenth century.

Morphology. This genus includes at least 350 species, all woody plants, quite varied in size, form and flower colour, and including a great number of horticultural species. They are shrubs ranging from 1 to 60 feet, evergreen or deciduous, with alternate, entire leaves.

Flowers are borne on pedicels, in terminal umbel-like racemes; the flower is rotate, bell-shaped or funnel-shaped, most often with five lobes, white or in any shade of rose, red, violet, yellow, or orange; the fruit is a capsule containing numerous seeds.

Varieties. Bailey, the authority on horticulture, distinguishes between rhododendrons, deciduous azaleas and Indian azaleas.

Rhododendrons are those plants that enrich the shrubberies, gardens and parks with their superb, abundant spring bloom and are ornamental for the rest of the year with their shiny, full foliage; among these the hybrids are the most numerous, including combinations of the North American, Himalayan, Sikh, and Chinese species.

Cultivation. The great ornamental quality of rhododendrons—which are slow-growing—is evident whether they are used as isolated specimens or in great masses; the dwarf species are suited to rock gardens and cliff plantings. In any case, these plants prefer mild winters, ample water, a humid atmosphere, light shade, protection from the wind and snow, and a soil rich in humus, cool, moderately-acid, and well drained. If the soil is alkaline add sulphur, peat moss, and leaf mould. The roots are very shallow and the soil must not be cultivated.

The rhododendrons transplant easily, provided they are moved with a ball of earth. Seed may be sown in pots in a mixture of peat and sand and covered lightly with sand or damp sphagnum. They may be propagated by cuttings of almost mature wood, or by division. Hybrids are grafted in winter in a warm greenhouse, on root-stock of *Rhododendron catawbiense*.

The deciduous azaleas, also used outdoors, flower from April to June, according to type. The Indian types are evergreen but must be kept in the greenhouse in winter.

Several insects and disease attack azaleas and rhododendrons, but most may be easily controlled. The most common problem with azaleas is chlorosis that develops in soils insufficiently acid. This may be corrected by spraying the plant with a ferrous solution.

143-148. Rhododendrons and azaleas have a large number of cultivars. Both the flowers and the foliage are ornamental.

145

146

147

144

148

Forsythia

Genus *Forsythia*, family Oleaceae

This genus comprises three species widely grown for the beauty of their flowers; *Forsythia suspensa*, *F. viridissima*, and hybrid *F. intermedia*.

Morphology. *F. suspensa*, a shrub which can grow to about 10 feet tall, has deciduous leaves; many slender, flexible, drooping branches; opposite, ovate, serrated leaves, often tripartite; bell-shaped flowers grouped in clusters at the nodes, deeply four-parted, bright golden yellow. This fruit is a capsule with winged seeds. The branches take root when they come into contact with the soil. Variety *Fortunei* is more erect with arching branches, is more vigorous, and has sulphur-yellow flowers with twisted petals.

F. viridissima differs in having erect branches, greenish-yellow flowers, and leaves toothed above the middle.

F. intermedia often has tripartite leaves and flowers like those of the variety *Fortunei*. A distinguishing characteristic among the three species is in the branches, hollow between the nodes in *F. suspensa*. There is layered pulp in the other two species, absent in the nodes of *F. intermedia* and present in the nodes of *F. viridissima*. *F. intermedia* has an excellent variety, *spectabilis*, whose flowers are more numerous, more colourful and larger than any other of the genus.

Origin. Both *F. suspensa* and *F. viridissima* are native to China.

Cultivation. These are shrubs adapted to any type of soil if not too compact and dry; they prefer a south or west wall or a sheltered shrubbery. Forsythias are valued for their abundant, showy bloom along the whole branch, which appears early (from March to April), before the leaves. These plants may also be forced in the greenhouse. They are propagated by division in September, by cuttings, or layering. They should be pruned heavily just after flowering.

The foliage is not attacked by insects, but is infected by disease; a blistering of the stem, a root rot, and two kinds of wilt may be problems.

152

153

154

Viburnum

Genus *Viburnum*, family Caprifoliaceae
The name of the genus is the old Latin name.

Morphology. The viburnums comprise a large group of about 120 species having in common the following characteristics: leaves almost always deciduous, opposite, most often entire; small flowers in dense terminal panicles or umbel-like cymes; fruit a single-seeded drupe, often of a vivid colour.

The species most often grown in gardens for its bloom is the Snowball, (*Viburnum Opulus* var. *roseum*), named for the large spring inflorescence, which is spherical, formed only of sterile flowers, and of large size. The flowers are limited to the outer part of the inflorescence which is globular. The leaves are tri-lobed. The fruit is bright red; the leaves become purple in autumn. It is a deciduous variety.

Other species. Rather widespread in the Mediterranean region, most suitable for hedges, the Laurestinus (*Viburnum Tinus*) has leathery evergreen, oval, and shiny leaves and white or pinkish flowers in summer.

The common deciduous *V. Lantana*, or Wayfaring-Tree, is suited for rock gardens; it has white flowers. Fruit is red, turning black.

The *V. Rhytidophyllum* is evergreen and has long, dense, reticulate leaves, dark green and shiny on top, whitish and tomentose underneath, with white flowers.

Probably the most beautiful deciduous flowering viburnum is *V. Carlesii*, a native of Korea. It is a shrub with numerous stiff branches, about 4 feet tall, with a down of stellate hairs on the young branches and on both sides of the leaves. The leaves are ovate, acute, and irregularly toothed. The flowers are clustered in semiglobular cymes, rose-coloured or white, and fragrant.

Cultivation. With the exception of the snowball and *V. Lantana*, all the viburnums prefer a cool soil and semi-shade. Dry positions should be avoided, and older specimens must not be overcrowded. Weak shoots must be removed in winter.

The viburnums are grown as isolated specimens, in clumps and in hedges for their flowers, their coloured fruit, and their foliage. Propagation is by seed after stratification. The evergreen kinds may be propagated by softwood cuttings in summer under glass, half-ripened shoots being inserted in sandy loam in gentle bottom heat in July and August. All may be propagated by division. The varieties with sterile flowers are grafted on *V. Opulus* or *V. Lantana* or propagated by cuttings.

149, 151. *Forsythia intermedia* in flower.

150. *Chaenomeles lagenaria* cultivar Rowallane (Japanese Flowering Quince).

152. Inflorescence of a viburnum.

153. Inflorescence of *Viburnum Carlesii*.

154. Fruit of *Viburnum Opulus*.

155

Foliage shrubs

Pittosporum

Pittosporum Tobira, family Pittosporaceae
The name of the genus comes from the Greek, meaning "resinous seed", it being covered with a sticky substance; *Tobira* is the Japanese name of this species.

Morphology. This is an evergreen shrub or small tree, which reaches a height of about 10 feet, with a twisted trunk covered with a smooth bark, having a globular form, with obovate, obtuse leaves narrowing to a wedge on a short petiole. The leaves are dense and leathery, smooth, dark green and shiny on top; their edges are entire and down-curved; leaves are alternate, appearing in whorls on the twigs.

The small flowers are white or greenish, with a strong fragrance resembling orange blossoms, in terminal panicles and appearing during winter in the south, or in spring. The fruits are ovoid capsules densely covered with short hairs. The variety *variegata* has leaves variegated with white.

Origin. This plant is native to China and Japan.

Cultivation. In Europe this shrub is widely grown along the Mediterranean coast, to whose climate it adapts because it tolerates summer drought and thrives on mild winters and is resistant to winds carrying salt spray. In Britain

156   157

it can be grown in the open in the warmest maritime regions of the south-west. In less favoured zones it must be planted in the shelter of a wall and in a warm spot. It needs acid soil.

For greenhouse culture it should be potted March or April, and kept at 60° to 70°F until October and from 40° to 50°F until April. It is valued for the ornamental foliage and the fragrance of the flowers, as well as for its vigour.

Pittosporum can be propagated by seed, which is, however, difficult to preserve. Seed is sown in a cool greenhouse in spring. Cuttings of half-mature wood up to 3 inches long may be planted in small pots of sandy soil, under bell-glass at a temperature of around 60°F, in summer.

Other species. Other species sometimes cultivated, mostly native to Oceania, are *P. crassifolium* (Karo) and *P. tenuifolium* (Tawhiwhi) from New Zealand, with dark purple flowers; *P. erioloma* and *P. viridiflorum* are similar to *P. Tobira*; *P. undulatum* (Victorian Box), native to Australia, is sometimes used as the stock for grafting.

---

155. *Pittosporum Tobira* in a Mediterranean garden.

156, 157. *Pittosporum Tobira* in flower, and detail.

158. Inflorescence of *Prunus Laurocerasus*.

159. High hedge of *Prunus Laurocerasus*.

158

159

Cherry laurel

Prunus Laurocerasus, family Rosaceae
Laurocerasus indicates that the fruit somewhat resembles cherries while the evergreen leaves may be likened to those of the laurel.

Morphology. This is an evergreen shrub or small tree growing to 20 feet, with an irregular crown; smooth grey bark; leaves obovate or elliptical with a pointed tip, on a short petiole, thick and leathery, with almost entire edges, shiny dark green on top, dull, and lighter green beneath.

The flowers, small and white, open in the spring in erect racemes that are terminal or axillary to the leaves and have a pleasing odour of bitter almonds. The inedible fruit is ovoid, small, fleshy, purple; leaves are poisonous.

Varieties. The botanical varieties are numerous and differ principally in the form and size of the leaves; those with large leaves come from the Caucasus, those with small leaves from the Balkans. The variety *Caucasica* is a fine, large-leaved form; *schipkaensis* has a pyramidal habit and is very hardy; *magnoliaefolia* has leaves up to 12 inches long similar to those of the magnolia; *rotundifolia* leaves are short and obtuse, a good hedging variety.

Origin. In nature this plant lives in cool areas; it is considered, like box, a species of Tertiary origin, at one time spread through other parts of Europe, as fossil remains show, and driven back to the places where it is found naturally today by Quaternary glaciers.

Cultivation. The cherry laurel is frequently employed for high hedges, fences, and espaliers which may be moderately pruned; it also adapts to planting in tubs for indoor use. It is propagated by cuttings of mature wood inserted in sheltered borders or cold frames in autumn. New varieties are grown by seeds. Pruning to shorten straggly growths is done in April.

Other species. A somewhat related species is *P. lusitanica* (Portugal Laurel) of the Iberian peninsula and the Canary Islands, useful for hedging, with shiny, persistent leaves, and its varieties *azorica* with large leaves and *variegata* with leaves margined silver. A lesser known variety is *myrtifolia* that is notable for its dense form.

60

Holly

Ilex Aquifolium, family Aquifoliaceae

Morphology. The Common holly is a true tree, although cultivated specimens are for the most part bushy. The crown is dense with leathery, evergreen leaves dark and shiny on top, dull and lighter on the underside, ovate, mostly with coarse spiny teeth.

The flowers are small, white or somewhat pink, in axillary cymes on last year's growth; the plant is ordinarily dioecious; the fruits are shiny red berries. It is native to Europe, particularly Britain.

Varieties. *Heterophylla* has leaves entire; *pendula* has pendulous branches; *pyramidalis* is an excellent variety for berries; *variegata* has leaves mottled with silver and gold; *ferox* (Hedgehog Holly) is prickly also on the top side of the leaf; *bacciflava* has yellow berries.

Cultivation. Holly prefers a cool, humid climate and acid soil. It is suitable for hedges since it is easy to shape, and the berries persist part of the winter.

Holly is propagated by seeds stratified after the fleshy portion is removed; the varieties are propagated by grafting or by cuttings of mature wood. This method serves to ensure that female plants will be obtained. When transplanting, it should be moved with a root ball.

Other species. *I. opaca* is the native American holly. *I. crenata* is the Japanese holly; *I. cornuta* is the Chinese holly. Greenhouse species cultivated include *I. Cassine* native to America, and *paraguariensis*, "Paraguay Tea" from Brazil. *Euonymous japonicus* belongs to a related family (Celastraceae). It is evergreen, spreading, with oval, shiny leaves, edged with small, obscure teeth, in some varieties marbled or edged with golden yellow. Frequently used in borders is the evergreen *Aucuba japonica*, often with marbled yellow leaves tolerant of shade.

160, 162. *Ilex Aquifolium* in a form with marginate leaves.

161. Berries of *Ilex Aquifolium*.

163. *Aucuba japonica*.

164. *Euonymus japonicus* with variegated foliage.

160

161

162

163

164

165

166

Box

Buxus sempervirens, family Buxaceae
The genus name was in use among the early Romans. *Sempervirens* means "evergreen".

Morphology. This is a hardy evergreen shrub with small stiff leaves, at the most 20 feet tall, but along the Black and Caspian seas it becomes a true tree. The trunk is covered with light, scaly bark; leaves are dense, small, oval, opposite, entire, almost sessile, leathery, dark green and shiny on top.

The spring flowers are yellowish, small, grouped in axillary clusters. The fruit is a capsule. The presence of alkaloids makes box a poisonous plant, and no part of it should be eaten.

Varieties. The most widely cultivated species are *B. balearica* native to the Balearic Islands, 8 feet; and *B. sempervirens* varieties such as *argenteo-variegata*, *angustifolia*, *marginata*, *glauca*, *rotundifolia*, *rosmarinifolia*, *myrtifolia* (dwarf with narrow leaves), and *bullata* (with bulbous leaves). *B. microphylla*, 3 feet, is native to Japan, and its variety *japonica* has various forms.

Origin. Box is native to the chains of the Atlas Mountains, and European regions with a Mediterranean, sub-Mediterranean, or Atlantic climate; usually it occurs in rocky areas or in shady undergrowth. It is not associated with any particular soil but is usually found in limestone soils in Europe. *B. microphylla* is usually found in acid soils in Japan. All varieties are slow growing, although some grow more rapidly than others.

Cultivation. Box is used to make dense hedges that may be pruned to any form, and the dwarf varieties are used for edging. It is valued for its adaptability to shade. It is drought-resistant and should always be in well-drained soil.

---

165. Detail of *Buxus sempervirens*.

166. *Buxus balearica*.

Privet

Ligustrum ovalifolium, family Oleaceae

The name of the genus is an ancient Latin term; that of the species indicates the leaf form.

Morphology. This privet is a large semi-evergreen shrub or small tree extending up to 15 feet tall, with smooth, opposite, ovalelliptical, thick, entire, dark green leaves, shiny on top, sometimes purple in autumn.

The small white flowers appear in June or July, have four petals, are in panicles and have a strong fragrance; the fruit are blackberry-like drupes.

Varieties. Of cultivated varieties, the following are interesting: *aureo-marginatum* (leaves edged with yellow), *variegatum* (with yellow-marbled leaves), *tricolor* (leaves variegated white and yellowish, pink when young), *multiflorum* (flowering abundantly), and *lucidum* with broad, lustrous foliage that grows to 18 feet.

Origin. This species is native to Japan. It may be planted in any soil. It is of no great ornamental value.

Because privet is chiefly used for hedging in Britain it has become susceptible to a number of root diseases including white root rot which is usually confined to the south-west of England. In the north of England a fungi *Verticullum dahliae* has been found on the roots of privet. Dieback and canker of privet twigs has been reported as being caused by *Glomerella cingulata* which is responsible for Bitter rot of apples.

Cultivation. It tolerates drought, salt, and a certain amount of shade. It grows rapidly. It is used to create hedges (it may be pruned to any shape), as centres of flower beds, and as single specimens. Propagation is by hardwood or softwood cuttings, by division or by seed. Varieties are grafted on the type species. Cuttings should be about 9 to 12 inches in length, planted outdoors from late August to November in a shady position.

Other species. A related species also grown for hedges is *Ligustrum vulgare* (common privet), widespread in Britain, distinguishable by its smaller leaves, deciduous and less pointed, and by its small stature. It is hardier than *L. ovalifolium*. This privet also has many varieties, including *buxifolium* (semipersistent, obtuse leaves), *glaucum* (leaves edged in white), *atrovirens* (with narrow leaves, almost persistent), *pendulum*, *pyramidale* (habit pyramidal), *chlorocarpum*, *leucocarpum*, *xanthocarpum* (respectively with greenish, white, and yellow fruit), *aureum* (leaves yellow), and others.

---

167. Inflorescence of *Ligustrum ovalifolium*.

168. Privet pruned to ornamental shapes.

169. A species of pyracantha with yellow fruit.

170. A form of pyracantha with orange fruit.

171. Detail of *Pyracantha coccinea*.

172. *Crataegus Oxyacantha* var. *coccinea*.

167

168

Fruiting shrubs

Pyracantha

Pyracantha coccinea, family Rosaceae
The generic name derives from the Greek words *pyr*, "fire", and *acantha*, "thorn". *Coccineus*, in Latin, means "red". The common name is "firethorn".

Morphology. This is a handsome evergreen shrub up to 20 feet tall, with small, alternate, oval-oblong leaves, shallowly-toothed or in some cases entire, stipulate, thick, and shiny green. The branches are spiny.

The flowers are small, white, and numerous in corymbs during May and June; fruits are small round pomes in red, orange, or yellow.

Varieties. The variety *Lalandii* is hardier and has broader clusters and orange-rose fruits; *crenulata*, Nepalese White Thorn, grows up to 15 feet and needs wall protection; its variety *Rogersiana* has glossy foliage and orange fruits.

Origin. The shrub is native to Southern Europe and Asia Minor. The variety *Lalandii* comes from central and western China.

Cultivation. It prefers a well-drained soil and thrives on acid or limestone soil. It is propagated by seed, by cuttings of mature wood kept in a moderately warm greenhouse, by division, and sometimes by grafting on hawthorn or cotoneaster.

It is well adapted to rocky slopes and to shrub borders and makes an excellent hedge.

Other species. Other cultivated kinds are *Pyracantha crenato-serrata* with coral-red fruit, native to China, and *P. angustifolia*, also from China, with narrow leaves and orange fruit.

169

171

170

172

173

Cotoneaster

Genus *Cotoneaster*, family Rosaceae

Morphology. These are shrubs or, rarely, small trees, devoid of spines. They are deciduous or evergreen, with entire leaves.

The flowers are small, borne singly or in terminal cymes, white or pink, with five petals; the fruit is small, spherical, often red.

Species and varieties. The Chinese *Cotoneaster bullata* is a spreading bush, with few branches, growing to 6 feet. Leaves are rather large, deciduous, ovate, greyish-green underneath. The pinkish flowers appear in May and June and the fruits are bright red. The varieties *floribunda* and *macrophylla*, abundantly flowered, are very handsome.

C. acutifolia from Central China is a shrub of vigorous growth up to 10 feet with black fruit. Its variety *villosula* has leaves pubescent underneath.

C. Dielsiana, also from China, is a shrub growing up to 6 feet tall, with spreading and arching branches and small, deciduous, ovate to elliptical leaves and red fruit. The variety *elegans* has smaller, semipersistent leaves.

C. horizontalis is prostrate, with distichous branches covering the ground; in autumn the leaves turn yellow first, then red, falling off the shrub quite late; the abundant fruits are ovoid and red. The variety *perpusilla* has very small leaves.

C. Conspicua var. *decora* is another prostrate form bearing many berries.

Also native to China, *C. salicifolia* is evergreen or nearly so, up to 15 feet tall, with elliptical-oblong to ovate-lanceolate leaves that are acute, rough, and glabrous on top; the fruit is a bright red.

C. integerrima, suited to rock gardens, has deciduous foliage, downy underneath, and red fruits. *C. microphylla*, 2 feet, trailing is suitable for walls and rockeries. *C. tomentosa* with obtuse leaves is native to Europe and is particularly adapted to limestone soils. Since hybridization is easy in this genus, numerous hardy cultivars have been developed, with coloured autumn foliage.

C. Watereri is a vigorous free-fruiting hybrid, growing to 15 feet. *Zabelii* with purple pear-shaped berries, originating in China, grows to 6 feet.

Cultivation. The cotoneasters prefer well-drained soil and full sun. They are at their best as colour highlights and, especially in their prostrate forms, adorning rock gardens. The fruit, persisting part of the winter, is rather decorative. Propagation is by seed sown 1 inch deep outdoors in March. The evergreen species may be propagated by cuttings of half-mature wood inserted in sandy soil in frames in September, and by grafting on *C. integerrima*, and by division.

173. A cotoneaster, with fruit.

174. *Cotoneaster integerrima.*